Aboriginal Men of High Degree

Aboriginal Men of High Degree

Initiation and Sorcery in the World's Oldest Tradition

A. P. ELKIN

Inner Traditions
Rochester, Vermont

Inner Traditions International
One Park Street
Rochester, Vermont 05767
www.InnerTraditions.com

First published by the University of Queensland Press,
St. Lucia, Queensland, Australia

Library of Congress Cataloging-in-Publication Data

Elkin, A. P. (Adolphus Peter), 1891–1979
Aboriginal men of high degree: initiation and sorcery in the world's oldest tradition / A. P. Elkin.
p. cm.
Originally published: 2nd ed. St. Lucia, Queensland: Queensland University Press, 1978, c1977.
Includes bibliographical references and index.
ISBN 0-89281-421-7
1. Australian aborigines—Medicine. 2. Shamans—Australia. 3. Australian aborigines—Religion. I. Title.
GN666.E3 1994
299'.92—dc20 93-30461
CIP

Printed and bound in the United States

10 9 8 7 6 5 4

Text design by Electric Dragon Productions

Contents

Foreword

Aboriginal Men of High Degree was first published in 1945, three years after I was born. As a Tasmanian Aborigine, from a younger generation than those who are the subject of this book, I do not in any way question the validity of what Professor Elkin has written or recorded about Australian Aborigines who are not from Tasmania, nor do I confirm or reject his details. Our spiritual perspective is not based on universal doctrines but is related to and respectful of specific groups whose origins are specific land areas. Should there be inaccuracies or misinterpretations by Elkin, then it is for representatives of the people he describes to state their views on his writings. For all of us, however, *Aboriginal Men of High Degree* gives an insight into how white society perceives the mystic, spiritual, and psychic world of Aboriginal people. It shows too the inability of the Western world, which has lost contact with its indigenous mentality and its spiritual world, to participate in the Spirit–human interaction.

Professor Elkin made many surveys of Aboriginal society. From 1927 to 1972 he devoted much effort to the study of Aboriginal customs relating to the powers of Aboriginal men of high degree. Much of what Professor Elkin has written in this book may appear too mystic or too ritualistic to be accepted as fact. He makes his own statements about the views that place doubt on the powers of Aboriginal men to go beyond what Western civilization accepts as reality. He provides an opportunity for Aboriginal people to view their culture through the eyes of an alien society, as well as for whites to glimpse a society that must appear even more alien to them. Professor Elkin tries to come to terms with the unknown. In a way, he expresses an ingenuous understanding of the phenomenon of Aboriginality as it once existed, unadulterated by magic or cultural tricksterism. For the keen observer, his account weaves a story of a lost civilization;

for the knowing, it welds one reality with another reality. Unfortunately, Aboriginal men of high degree are seen by Elkin to be taking a final bow, to be engaged in the ultimate disappearing act from the human world. The impact of Western society has forced the Aboriginal medicine men to become "outdated."

My view, however, is more positive. It embraces the world we now know and concepts and perspectives, from the spiritual to the sociopolitical, that can be seen as unique in Aboriginality. We as contemporary Aborigines, as well as all inhabitants of a troubled society and environment, will do well to maintain them.

Today's Aboriginal society maintains a knowledge of the "Featherfoot," the medicine men of tribal society, and of the powers practiced by those so chosen. Aboriginal men and women of high degree both exist in Australia's contemporary Aboriginal society. They are few, they are not powerful, and they do not fully explore their respective potentials. Yet, in a way, their aspirations in seeking to influence conscious attention to Aboriginal responsibilities are shared by the majority of Aboriginal people. Chosen Aboriginal people today receive messages from the Spirits in the form of animals or special elements of the land. The Tasmanian Aboriginal community has experienced spiritual messages as far back as I can recall. My grandfather told me of many spiritual messages of his lifetime, and stories he passed on from his parents and grandparents remind me that part of our ancient culture will "visit" us from time to time.

I remember most clearly the reburial ceremony held by the Tasmanian Aboriginal community for John Shinall, whose head was stolen from his grave by European scientists during the last century. We were able to influence the return of his human remains from the Royal Society in Ireland in 1992. The ceremony was held at Sorrell, Tasmania, outside Hobart, in 1993. Michael Mansell, Aboriginal lawyer and community leader, who actively achieved the return of John Shinall's preserved head, presided at the reburial. As he delivered his graveside address in our tribal language a black cockatoo (mennuggana) flew in from the west and landed on an old dead tree immediately above Michael. Mennuggana sat watching until Michael finished his address to the community mourners and then flew immediately off to the west. The Tasmanian Aboriginal people know mennuggana as the messenger bird.

On another occasion, at Oyster Cove, the Tasmanian Aboriginal community cremated our ancestors' human remains, which had been returned to us after an emotional campaign that forced the Tasmanian government to return those remains from both state museums in 1984. A stiff easterly wind was blowing as the cremation pyre was lit and the smoke billowed into the sky. But instead of going with the wind to the west, as it should have, the smoke went directly into the wind toward Bruny Island—the island where many of our ancestors had originated before their imprisonment at Oyster Cove late in the last century. There at Oyster Cove they all died some years later, and their graves were robbed. At Oyster Cove a hundred years later the return of the cremation smoke from their remains completed the cycle of their lives. The event was well observed by the Aboriginal people at the ceremony and was considered to be an acknowledgment of respect between the living and the dead.

I have felt the presence of our Spirits when visiting Kuti Kina cave in the southwest wilderness of Tasmania. Sitting by myself inside the damp, cold cave used by our Old People as long as 27,000 years ago, I began to feel a physical warmth creep over me. It became warmer, as if the sun had entered the cave. When I got up to leave, the warmth stayed with me until I reached the outside of the cave. I went away feeling the welcome of the Spirits inside me.

Changes that have been forced on the tradition of Aboriginal men of high degree have caused contemporary Australian Aboriginal society to adapt to the forceful powers of colonial oppression. The dominant white culture in Australia is based on a historical belief that Aborigines must be assimilated into the Australian culture. In 200 years we have seen Aboriginal religions, customs, languages, land management, and social cohesion calculatedly forced out of Australian Aborigine society. The view of whites has been, and continues to be, that Australians are one people and that Aborigines must be assimilated to remove the indigenous consciousness from the "new nation." The assimilation program has failed, but it is still a covert objective in the minds of the majority of Australians.

Aboriginal perspectives on spiritual knowledge in such areas as healing, death, punishment, magic, and interactive psychic and animistic beliefs are not clearly understood by white people. Even most Aboriginal people today do not understand them. Those who do have some grasp on Aboriginal spirituality to the depth of high degree are adapting that knowledge to a broader need in Aboriginal cultural maintenance.

Contemporary Aboriginal society is changing at an incredible pace. Its amalgamation with Western technologies and its yielding to social and cultural pressures create an immense threat to indigenous relationships with the world ecological order. Aboriginal people are in the throes of a political struggle to have their land and rights restored. As modern society intrudes into indigenous minds, introducing different values and directions, Aborigines can be expected to lose sight of certain principles in the process.

"Aboriginal land rights" does not mean that the people are simply entitled to land. Nor does the term mean that the land owes anything to the people. Aborigines do not justify land rights in terms of economy, accommodation, or possession. Rather, Aboriginal land rights represent a whole set of responsibilities, among which is the obligation to preserve the unique essence of their original law. Aborigines have the responsibility to be custodians of land, sea, and sky. They must remain accountable to the ecological world, which accepts indigenous intrusion and use of that ecology only on sound practices of interaction with the spirit of the land, manifested in strict rules of respect and protection.

Today, Aboriginal men and women of high degree, who understand their responsibilities as keepers of indigenous principles, can learn much from Professor Elkin's *Aboriginal Men of High Degree*—not about the tribal practice or mystical world of yesterday, but about the intangible accountability woven between the lines of this book. Elkin brings out the views but not the inner workings; Aboriginal people of high degree must seek the details for themselves, whether in the areas of healing, the law, the animistic meshing with people, or the rules of land management. In all those endeavors, the responsibilities of indigenous people of high degree can be carried with us as a symbol of human accountability in being allowed the right to participate in the planet's ecology. Undoubtedly, failure to achieve recognition and practice of indigenous principles will end this era of human life on planet Earth.

Jim Everett
Aboriginal Writer in Residence
Riawunna
Aboriginal Student Services
University of Tasmania
June 1993

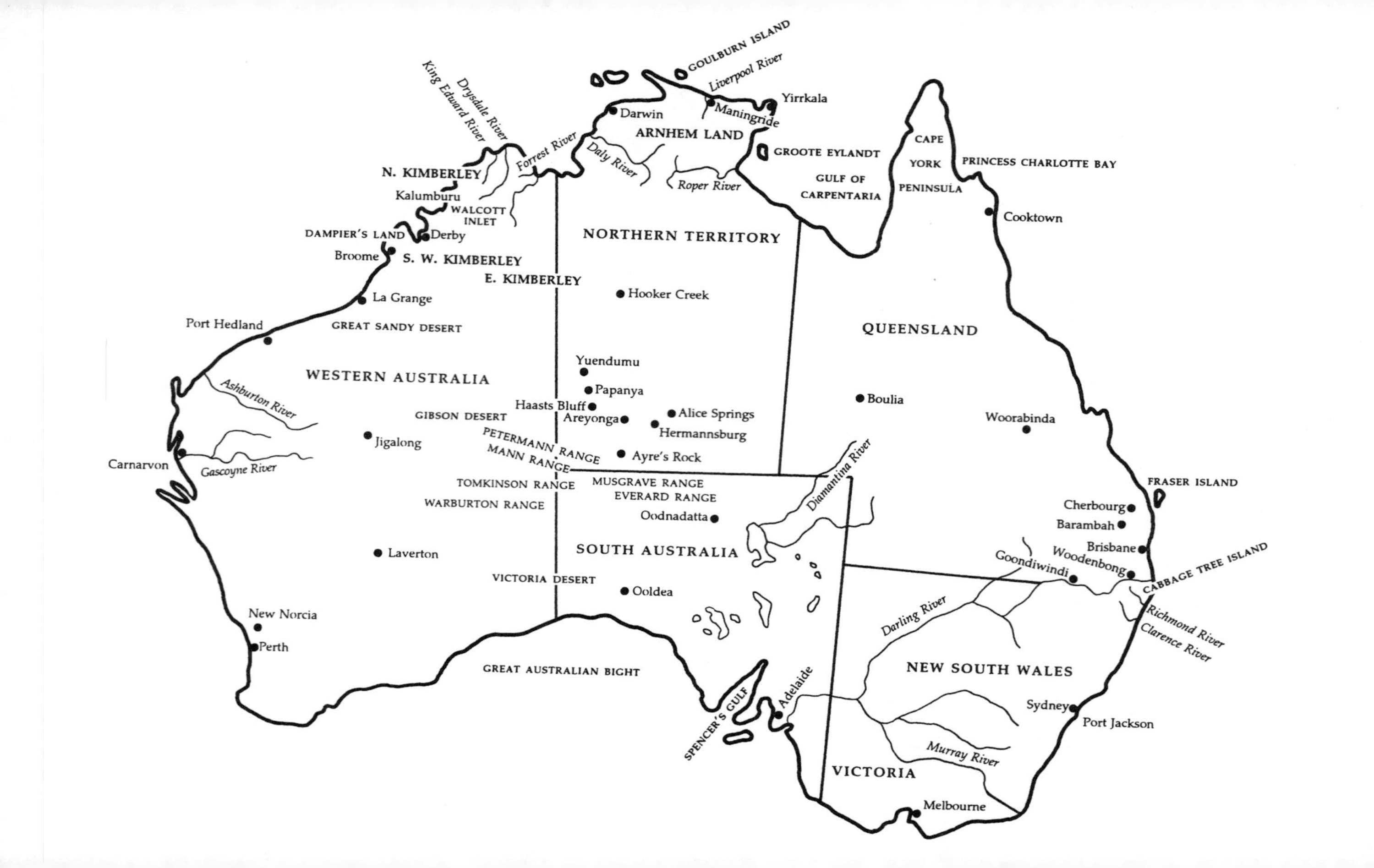
GOULBURN ISLAND
Liverpool River
Yirrkala
Maningride
Darwin
ARNHEM LAND
Drysdale River
King Edward River
Forrest River
Daly River
GROOTE EYLANDT
CAPE
YORK
PENINSULA
PRINCESS CHARLOTTE BAY
N. KIMBERLEY
Roper River
GULF OF
CARPENTARIA
Kalumburu
WALCOTT
INLET
Cooktown
DAMPIER'S LAND
Derby
NORTHERN TERRITORY
Broome
S. W. KIMBERLEY
E. KIMBERLEY
Hooker Creek
La Grange
Port Hedland
GREAT SANDY DESERT
QUEENSLAND
Yuendumu
WESTERN AUSTRALIA
Papanya
Boulia
Haasts Bluff
Alice Springs
Woorabinda
GIBSON DESERT
Areyonga
Ashburton River
Hermannsburg
Jigalong
PETERMANN RANGE
Diamantina River
MANN RANGE
Ayre's Rock
Carnarvon
Gascoyne River
TOMKINSON RANGE
MUSGRAVE RANGE
FRASER ISLAND
EVERARD RANGE
WARBURTON RANGE
Cherbourg
Oodnadatta
Barambah
SOUTH AUSTRALIA
Brisbane
Laverton
Goondiwindi
Woodenbong
VICTORIA DESERT
CABBAGE TREE ISLAND
Ooldea
Darling River
Richmond River
New Norcia
Clarence River
Perth
GREAT AUSTRALIAN BIGHT
NEW SOUTH WALES
Adelaide
Sydney
SPENCER'S GULF
Port Jackson
Murray River
VICTORIA
Melbourne

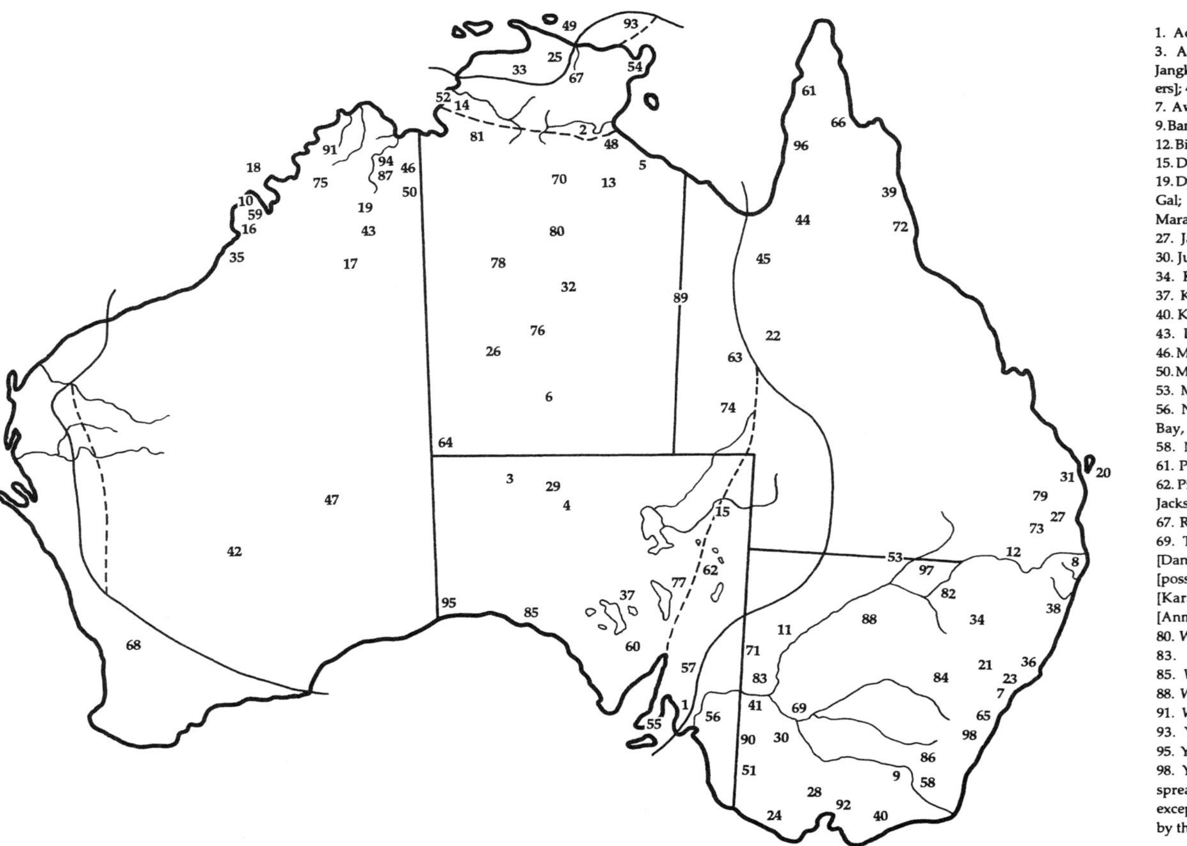

1. Adelaide Tribes [Kaurna, etc.]; 2. Alawa; 3. Aluridja Tribes [Antakerinya, Kokata, Jangkundjara, Ngalea, Wonggai, and some others]; 4. Antakerinya; 5. Anula; 6. Aranda [Arunta]; 7. Awabakal [Lake Macquarie]; 8. Bandjelang; 9. Bangerang; 10. Bard; 11. Barkinji [Wampangee]; 12. Bigumbal; 13. Binbinga; 14. Daly River Tribes; 15. Dieri; 16. Djaber-Djaber; 17. Djaru; 18. Djaui; 19. Djerag; 20. Fraser Island [Batjala]; 21. Geawe-Gal; 22. Goa [Koa]; 23. Gringai; 24. Gunditj-Mara; 25. Gunwinggu; 26. Ilpirra [Walpari]; 27. Jagara; 28. Jajauring; 29. Jakundja-djara; 30. Jupagalk; 31. Kabi; 32. Kaitish; 33. Kakadu; 34. Kamilaroi; 35. Karadjeri; 36. Kattang; 37. Kokata; 38. Kumbaingeri; 39. Kungganji; 40. Kurnai; 41. Laitu-Laitu; 42. Laverton Tribes; 43. Lunga; 44. Maikulan; 45. Maitakudi; 46. Malngin; 47. Manjindja; 48. Mara; 49. Maung; 50. Miriwun; 51. Mukjarawaint; 52. Mulukmuluk; 53. Murawari; 54. Murngin; 55. Narrang-ga; 56. Narrinyeri [Lower Murray and Encounter Bay, Jaralde and other tribes]; 57. Ngaduri; 58. Ngarigo; 59. Nyul-nyul 60. Pankala; 61. Pennefather River Tribes [Nggerikudi, etc.]; 62. Piladapa; 63. Pita-Pita; 64. Pitjintara; 65. Port Jackson Tribes; 66. Princess Charlotte Bay Tribes; 67. Rembarunga; 68. Southwest Corner W. A.; 69. Ta-Ta-Thi; 70. Tjingili; 71. Tongaranka [Danggali]; 72. Tully River Tribes; 73. Turrabal [possibly part of Jagara, No. 27]; 74. Ulupulu [Karanja]; 75. Ungarinyin; 76. Unmatjera [Anmatjera]; 77. Wailpi; 78. Walbiri; 79. Wakka; 80. Waramunga; 81. Wardaman; 82. Weilwan; 83. Wimbaio [Maraura], 84. Wiradjeri; 85. Wirangu; 86. Wolgal; 87. Wolyamidi; 88. Wongaibon; 89. Worgaia; 90. Wotjobaluk; 91. Wunambul; 92. Wurunjerri [Wurundjeri]; 93. Yaernungo; 94. Yeidji [Forrest River]; 95. Yerkla-Mining; 96. Yir-Yoront; 97. Yualai; 98. Yuin. (Continuous line indicates limits of spread of circumcision and also of subincision, except where the limits of the latter are indicated by the broken lines.)

Foreword to 1976 Edition

In 1944 Professor A. P. Elkin gave the John Murtagh Macrossan Memorial Lectures at the University of Queensland. These lectures along with two more chapters appeared in the following year as *Aboriginal Men of High Degree.* Published under wartime stringencies, the edition was a small one, which, nevertheless, circulated widely, becoming a major source for—among others—Mircea Eliade.[1] It has, however, been unobtainable for many years, and, despite the expansion of Aboriginal studies, it remains the only substantial work on what might be called the Aboriginal occult. With interest in the field now reviving, its publication is timely, the more so since the author, now Professor Emeritus, has written a new section.

Elkin's subject is the medicine man. But this term, with its connotations of chicanery and gullibility, scarcely conveys the importance such figures hold for Aborigines. The "clever man," as some English speakers call him, has acquired wonderful powers through direct contact with the beings of the dreamtime: the rainbow serpent, the sky gods, the spirits of the dead. He has come to this state through a long and rigorous apprenticeship and an initiation of terrors and ordeals beyond those that ordinary men undergo. He is what Elkin calls a man of high degree; his experiences have changed him utterly. He has died and come alive again; his entrails have been taken out and replaced; he has been swallowed by the rainbow serpent and regurgitated; magic crystals have been put in his body; he has acquired an animal familiar that dwells within him. As a result of such experiences, the medicine man can fly and travel over the ground at great speed; he can anticipate events and knows what is happening in faraway places. He can cure and kill mysteriously. He can make rain. He can ascend to the sky world on a magic cord that emanates from his testicles. He can roll in the fire without hurt, appear and disappear at will.

The man of high degree is not peculiar to Australia, of course. He is kindred to Carlos Castaneda's *brujo* Don Juan and other Amerindian "men of power."[2] The author himself draws parallels with the lamas of Tibet, anticipating Eliade's work on shamanism.[3] Eliade shows that it is not just the general phenomenon but numerous specific features that are to be found alike in Australia and Central Asia. But while Elkin believes that Aboriginal religion "belongs" to the Orient, not to the West, and allows the possibility of a historical connection, he is not inclined to the wide-ranging generalizations of comparative religion. His overriding purpose is to understand the Australian Aborigines.

Elkin will not allow the medicine men to be dismissed as frauds and humbugs, nor will he have them reduced to something else. He has been as unsympathetic to explanations in terms of the subconscious mind as he now is to the search for unconscious structures. He finds the notion that shamans are psychologically unstable equally inapplicable to Australia. Medicine men are part of the mainstream of Aboriginal society and culture, despite their absorption in the esoteric. The rigors of their "professional" training and the many ritual observances that surround its practice are, he thinks, enough to deter the mere eccentric as well as the confidence man.

It is, of course, always easier to explain away the occult than to explain it, and the difficulties are acute in the present case. For a start, we are almost wholly dependent on what the Aborigines tell us. Neither the author nor anyone else has tried, like Castaneda, to become the sorcerer's apprentice, and few whites can bear witness to the feats that are said to be performed. Elkin relays what he has been told, with the caution that one is probably never told everything.[4] But he wants the accounts to be taken seriously and approached with sympathetic understanding.[5]

Bolder than most anthropologists, Elkin is prepared to entertain the possibility that medicine men really have powers not understandable in terms of the rational and the academic. At one point he suggests that mass hypnosis may be the explanation for an extraordinary event. But he disclaims any special knowledge in this field, and thirty-one years later we are not much closer to an answer.[6] We might also talk in terms of "hallucinations" experienced during "abnormal states" such as trance. (Aborigines do not seem to use hallucinatory drugs.) But this approach begs the question of whether it is the "abnormal state" that induces the visions or the cultural milieu. Again we are in uncharted territory.

One possibility that Elkin does not explore is that some of the medicine man's marvels are deceptions, not in the fraudulent sense but the religious, what W. E. H. Stanner has called the "noble fiction." Lower-degree initiations are often conducted in this way: a boy is told that the roaring noise he hears is Daramulan coming to burn him to ashes before re-forming him. But when his eyes are unveiled, he discovers the bull-roarer; now he learns a more precious truth, that Daramulan's voice is "in the wood." The fiction is a secular screen for truths too sacred to be revealed to the uninitiated.[7] As Kenneth Maddock puts it, the novices are deceived only to be enlightened, and the outcome is not skepticism but faith.[8]

We do not know that the initiated medicine man has undergone this kind of "disillusioning" experience. As far as ordinary men are concerned, he has come face to face with the dreamtime beings, whom they have only encountered through symbols such as the bull-roarer. In this connection, Maddock has drawn an illuminating comparison between the Wiradjeri initiation myth and rite: whereas males originally were enlightened by Daramulan, later they were enlightened by their fellows.[9] The situation of the medicine man who is believed to have seen Baiame or been swallowed by the rainbow serpent replicates that of the dreamtime. It was perhaps in this sense that a Wongaibon described both the medicine men and the Crow of myth as "clever." Thus placed, the medicine men bear witness to the existence of the powers that their fellows experience only through symbols. If in fact their own experience is also through symbols, they keep it to themselves, carrying on behalf of the rest the knowledge that the dreamtime is after all inaccessible to mortals.

Although the medicine men are few in any community and stand apart from ordinary men, they are not rogues or mavericks. They do not have the marginal, even antisocial, character of the Melanesian sorcerer. They are part of the means by which the community maintains its connections with the powers that created the world and continue to sustain it. They are, as Elkin puts it, "a channel of life." In relation to the totemic and initiation rites, their role is complementary: for while the rites deal with general and continuing concerns, they deal with the particular and the contingent, with sickness, crime, dangers, separation, and the death of individuals. Moreover, their operations are what Stanner has called "transitive," in the sense that human intentions are—or seem to be—transferred to objects.[10] The rites are, in this sense, intransitive, depending on hope, belief, and faith, rather than perceivable results. But since the medicine men's feats derive from the same dreamtime powers, hope, belief, and faith are strengthened.

The book's first part is directed at the layman. In it Elkin is trying to communicate his own understanding of Aboriginal religion, in the hope that white Australians will come to appreciate it as something worthy of respect. As he says elsewhere, there are Aboriginal thinkers who "have caught a glimpse of, and attempted to grapple with, fundamental philosophical problems."[11]

The second part is more for the specialist. The author moves from the apt illustration of the first part to painstaking comparison of cognate phenomena across the continent. He draws on his field notebooks and those of his then research assistant, now Professor R. M. Berndt,[12] and on a wealth of published and unpublished data. Not the least virtue of this survey is the attention it gives to the distinctive and fascinating but often neglected cultures of southeastern Australia.

The third part, which Elkin has now added, brings to light data that have come to hand since the first edition. In particular it looks at Aboriginal men of high degree in the settings of mission and settlement and the context of cultural disintegration. The clever men of southeastern Australia have indeed vanished, and there is no possibility of their return. According to my own informants in western New South Wales, they were "too clever to live" and ended by killing one another, a verdict suggested by catastrophic population decline at a time of cultural collapse. Some lapsed into alcoholism, while others despaired as they found the younger generation unwilling or unfit to receive their knowledge. The half-caste Bandjigali, George Dutton, told me how, as a young drover, he had refused to take on the powers of a dying uncle. Riding home that night, he saw the euro that was the old man's familiar accompanying him along a stretch of road then turning off into the darkness.

In the Center, however, things are different. On the basis of recent reports, Elkin now thinks that the obituary he wrote for the medicine man was premature. He notes an interesting division of labor between black and white medicine men in some places and goes on to suggest that the former may still have a significant role to play in the outstation movement.

When *Aboriginal Men of High Degree* first appeared, there was little likelihood that Aborigines would read it. The few who had been educated to read such a book had also learned to be ashamed of their heritage. Today the situation is different, and I hope that this book, free as it is of technicalities and jargon, may enable some to reestablish the link.

Jeremy Beckett
Sydney 1976

Notes

1. See particularly Mircea Eliade, *Shamanism: Archaic Techniques of Ecstasy,* translated by W. R. Trask (Princeton N.J.: Princeton University Press, 1964). Mircea Eliade, *Australian Religions: An Introduction* (Ithaca, N.Y.: Cornell University Press, 1973).
2. See Carlos Castaneda, *The Teachings of Don Juan—A Yaqui Way of Knowledge* (Harmondsworth: Penguin, 1970), also three further volumes.

3. Eliade, *Shamanism*.
4. Elsewhere Elkin has written: "It is difficult to obtain complete knowledge of the initiation of adult males into full membership of their secret life. Judging from fresh bits of information that I acquire from time to time, I doubt whether we have, in any one instance, been admitted into all the secrets of the ritual and knowledge. But if this is difficult, it is more so when we come to inquire into that ritual through which a medicine man acquired power. Those who are not members of this profession know little about it." *The Australian Aborigines: How to Understand Them*, 4th edition (Sydney: Angus & Robertson, 1964), p. 325.
5. Elsewhere Elkin writes: "The anthropological field worker who has a sympathetic understanding of Christian or other religious groups cannot fail to regard Australian Aboriginal cults as religious. Certainly no member of such an esoteric society as the Masonic, which claims to rest on religious foundations, could deny it." "Religion and Philosophy of the Australian Aborigines" in *Essays In Honour of G. W. Thatcher*, ed. E. C. B. MacLaurin (Sydney: Sydney University Press, 1967), pp. 19–44.
6. At least one attempt has been made to test extrasensory perception among Aborigines: see W. A. McElroy, "Psi-Testing in Arnhemland," *Oceania* 26 (1955–56).
7. See R. H. Mathews, "The Burbung of the Wiradthuri Tribes," *Journal of the Royal Anthropological Institute* 25, 26 (1896, 1897). The writer recorded a similar account from a Wongaibon informant in 1957.
8. Kenneth Maddock, *The Australian Aborigines: A Portrait of Their Society* (Harmondsworth: Penguin, 1972), p. 115.
9. Maddock, *Australian Aborigines*, pp. 116–17.
10. W. E. H. Stanner, "On Aboriginal Religion, Part 1," *Oceania* 30 (1959): 124–27.
11. Elkin in *Essays in Honour of G. W. Thatcher*, p. 41.
12. Berndt subsequently published his own findings in two fascinating articles, "Wuradjeri Magic and 'Clever Men,' " Part I, *Oceania* 17 (1946–47), and Part II, *Oceania* 18 (1947–48).

Introduction to 1976 Edition

Thirty-one years have gone by since the first edition of this book was published. In the meantime more and fuller information on the making and powers of "Men of High Degree" has become available, especially for the Kimberley Division of Western Australia and the New South Wales north coast.

Further, a significant change has been occurring recently in the attitudes of some welfare and health agencies, official and nonofficial, toward medicine men. Where this is so, they are no longer ignored as men without knowledge or brushed aside as impostors. On the contrary, their age-old "professional" contribution to the well-being of their people is recognized, and their cooperation in official health services is asked for and is given, though somewhat tentatively on both sides.

For these reasons I have added part 3 to this new edition. Its main theme is the role of medicine men in the Aborigines' rapidly changing world. In 1945, the depopulation of full-blood Aborigines, which began in 1788, was continuing, and their extinction in the not-far-off future seemed inevitable. By the 1950s, however, the tide had turned, and both they and Aborigines of "mixed blood" were definitely increasing. Therefore, problems connected with their health, social conditions, and economic needs could no longer be allowed to drift but had to be tackled seriously, above all with the help of the Aborigines themselves. So governments have set up Aboriginal councils, boards, and committees on various aspects and interests of their life, giving them opportunity for self-determination and for exercising responsibility.

Accordingly, I refer to the relevance and role of Aboriginal medicine men in this new age: Is their role finished, as was thought by many even only a decade ago? If not, will they remain in an Order that is characterized by symbolical and mystic aspects, or will they become trained nursing aides and medical assistants in Aboriginal clinics and hospitals? The answers will be given by the Aborigines themselves.

To discuss these questions, I suggest at the end of the book that a conference be arranged of medicine men and some elders drawn from a widespread intertribal range of communities. It would be held preferably in a settlement away from townships, be run by the medicine men, and be subject to adjournments. This third suggestion is to ensure that the various communities and "tribes" can feel and think their way through the implications of any decision the conference might propose.

As the 1944 lectures from which this book grew were given on a University of Queensland Foundation, I welcome the publication of the new edition by the University of Queensland Press. The original was well received, but its selling price, as a first edition, has long since gone beyond the pockets of students and most general readers. In spite of this, requests for the book have been constant.

I thank persons far afield who have corresponded with me on aspects of the subject. They have included Dr. Dayalan Devanesen (Alice Springs), Mrs. Mary Laughren (Yuendumu), the Reverend L. Reece (Warrabri and Alice Springs), Mr. E. Evans (Darwin), and Mr. H. H. J. Coate (Derby).

Continuous and ever-watchful help has been given me by Mrs. Betty Dunne, secretary of "my" Department of Oceania Publications, University of Sydney, in library search as well as with typing and retyping. I thank her very sincerely as I do also Mrs. Joyce Beaumont, assistant in the same department, for her ready cooperation in many tasks, especially in the preparation of the maps.

Finally, I thank Dr. Jeremy Beckett of the Department of Anthropology, University of Sydney, for his furtherance of the project and particularly for writing the preface.

A. P. Elkin
Department of Oceania Publications
The University of Sydney
1976

Introduction to First Edition

The term *medicine man* as applied to Aboriginal Australia is used in a wide sense. Medicine men are leeches, in that they use objective means for the curing of illnesses and wounds. They are magical practitioners, for they cure some sicknesses by magical rituals and spells. In many parts they are sorcerers as well; they know how to, and may, insert evil magic, extract "human fat," or cause the soul to leave the victim's body, bringing about sickness and death. And finally, they also possess, in many cases, occult powers: they can commune with the dead; they see spirits fly through the air and do the same themselves; they go up to the sky; they practice telepathy and mass hypnotism; and they gain knowledge by psychical means of what occurs at a distance. Such are the claims and beliefs. They therefore partake of the character of witches, clairvoyants, mediums, and psychic experts.

The very existence of such powers suggests that mere instruction in leech-craft or indeed in the use of magical substances is not sufficient to make a person a medicine man. He possesses or is endowed with powers concerned with much else besides causing and curing illness. And even with regard to this, the Aborigines insist that the possession of such supernormal powers is the basis of the medicine man's curative efforts. He is a person of high degree, and not merely a member of a profession; he is a "clever man"—one who has been admitted to the secrets not disclosed to the ordinary, though fully initiated, man. Moreover, the admission to such knowledge and the ritual endowment with life are the necessary prelude to the exercise of supernormal and magical powers.

A survey of the rites of the making of medicine men reveals the type of ritual deemed essential and the powers with which they are endowed. We have information, often inadequate, for about eighty tribes. The inadequacy of the information is not surprising, seeing that the investigator must be on very confidential terms with the medicine man before the latter can be expected to impart his knowledge and beliefs and to describe his experiences. Moreover, a sound knowledge of the native language is desirable, if not essential. Unfortunately, very little attention has been paid to the medicine men, possibly because the prevailing concept of the inferiority of the Aborigines did not lead anyone to expect that any individuals would be worth study and understanding. In any case, native doctors were too often simply passed off as old rogues. Not even did Spencer and Gillen's interesting descriptions of medicine men in their books on the native tribes of Central and North-central Australia and the useful suggestions in A. W. Howitt's *Native Tribes of South-East Australia* inspire workers to probe deeply into this field. In recent years, Dr. W. L. Warner, Mr. R. H. Berndt, and myself have paid some attention to the subject, and I hope that the publication of these lectures will result in more attention being paid to this sphere of native life. If this occurs, I trust that the chancellor and senate of the University of Queensland will feel that their selection of the John Murtagh Macrossan Lecturer for 1944 was worthwhile.

For my own part, I considered that the best way to show my appreciation of the honor conferred on me by the University of Queensland was to select a field in which much research is required and one that is of absorbing human interest.

Chapters 1 and 2 are the lectures as delivered, with a few additions. Chapters 3 and 4 consist of a survey of our present knowledge of the making and powers of Aboriginal medicine men and provide the background of material for the actual lectures. But the importance of "men of high degree" and of psychic practices in Aboriginal life was brought home to me during fieldwork experience in several parts of Australia. Without that experience, these lectures would not have been given.

I would like to express my thanks to the vice-chancellor and members of the Professional Board of the University of Queensland and to Mr. T. Thatcher, secretary of the Public Lectures

Committee, for their hospitality and kindness to me during my visit to Brisbane for the purpose of delivering the lectures.

I also thank Mr. R. M. Berndt for making special investigations for me into the subject of these lectures and putting the results at my disposal; and Miss Jean Craig, teaching fellow in my own department, for her constant and ever-ready help in the preparation of this book for publication.

A. P. Elkin
Department of Anthropology
University of Sydney
January 1945

PART I

The Personality, Making, and Powers of Aboriginal Men of High Degree

CHAPTER 1

Aboriginal Men of High Degree: Their Personality and Making

Aboriginal Life—A Progress in Knowledge

Everywhere in Aboriginal Australia the young male, on approaching or reaching puberty, leaves behind him the interests of childhood. Henceforth, he speaks and thinks more and more as a man. In an unforgettable ceremonial manner, he is taken from the camp and scenes of his irresponsible early years. He becomes the subject of a series of rites, extending with intervals over several years. The trials that he undergoes and the operations performed on him vary in different parts of the continent. But the general pattern and purpose of the ritual are the same. He "dies" to the former life of childhood and of ignorance of esoteric knowledge and "rises" or is "reborn" to a new life. The latter is not merely adult life, for which he has meanwhile been disciplined and instructed. It is much more: it is a life of knowledge and power. At the end of the ritual journey, with its trials, loneliness, "death," revelations, and rejoicing, he can say: "Whereas previously I was blind to the significance of the seasons, of natural species, of heavenly bodies, and of man himself, now I begin to see; and whereas before I did not understand the secret of life, now I begin to know."

The word "secret" is used advisedly. Understanding of life and man is reserved for the initiated, for those who have successfully passed through various degrees. There are several of these, each of which is marked by its own ritual, name, and portion of esoteric knowledge. At various stages in his progress, after due warning and preparation and when in a condition of heightened suggestibility, the novice is shown sacred symbols (*tjurunga*) of wood or stone, secret ceremonies, and sacred rites; he hears sacred chants and is given some intimation of the significance and wonder of what he has seen and heard.

He does not see or learn everything at one time, or even during the main series of initiation rites. There is so much to know that many years are needed. Moreover, it must be learned word- and action-perfect, for the purpose is not simply to interest the "new man" and to enhance his personality, but also to preserve the sacred heritage, and to ensure the future of the tribe. For what is revealed to him is the complex of rites, chants, sacred sites, myths, and sanctions of behavior on which its life and future are believed to depend. This is usually summed up in one word, such as Altjiringa, Djugur, Bugari, Unggud, or Maratal of the Aranda, Aluridja, Karadjeri, Ungarinyin, or Wiradjeri tribes respectively. This word signifies the "eternal dreamtime," which is both a time and a state of life. It denotes the time and the power of the tribal cult-heroes, who are still present, though they performed their mighty works in the long-past. Moreover, the "dreamtime" and its heroes are the source of life in man and nature. Therefore, to be brought into full realization of the Altjiringa is to share actively in that stream of life and power that is not hampered by the limitations of space and time.

A man grows in knowledge by attending initiations and various cult-ceremonies and by learning from the "masters." Eventually he plays a leading part in the dreamtime rituals, on sacred ground, painted with arm blood or red ochre sanctified by the chanting that accompanies its application, and carrying or beholding the sacred symbols. On these occasions it is realized by both himself and all present that he is no longer himself; he is the great dreamtime hero whose role he is re-enacting, if only for a few minutes.

The function and purpose of these rituals are complex. They serve to strengthen in all present the realization of the dreamtime and the presence and power of its cult-heroes. They also dramatically remind and impress everyone present with all the sanctity and authority of traditional tribal behavior. In some cases, too, they are believed to cause the natural species to increase in their wonted way, so that man may live. But in addition to these effects, the rituals, with their dreamtime heroic associations, create and maintain in the participants unity of emotion, thought, and action; they renew sentiments that make for social continuity and cohesion; and so they bring about a highly desirable condition of social well-being and individual certainty and courage.[1]

The Problems of Daily Life

Initiation into the secret and sacred ritual and mythology of the tribe provides an authoritative background, a solid footing, and a sure hope for life. It gives general support and guidance to man in most moral and social situations. But it does not help him to cope specifically with the problems, desires, and setbacks of daily life, for example:

1. misfortune; bad luck; lack of success in love, hunting, or fighting; illness; or death;
2. lack of knowledge of what is occurring out of sight and at

a distance that may affect us unless we are forewarned and can take precautions;

3. ignorance of what the spirits of the dead or mischievous or evil spirits are likely to work on us;
4. the desire to obtain this or that object or goal, the realization of which is fraught with various uncertainties and contingencies.

In Aboriginal life these problems, setbacks, and desires are met in two ways. The first is the way of magic, with its rites, spells, paraphernalia, and concentration of thought. If it is designed to cause injury to an individual or social group, it is called black magic or sorcery; but if it is used to prevent evil or to produce good or well-being, it is called white magic.

The second way of meeting life's problems leads to the realm of psychic powers (and presumed psychic powers): hypnotism, clairvoyance, mediumship, telepathy, telesthesia, and the conquest of space and time.

All persons can, and indeed do, possess to a degree some of these powers. For example, in most tribes everybody can practice some forms of black magic and through dreams and traditionally formalized systems of presentiments know or learn what is happening at a distance that is of significance to themselves and their friends. Thus, to see in a vision of the night a person's dream totem (that is, the natural species or phenomenon that is his symbol in dreams) is to know that something is to happen to him or be done by him in relation to the dreamer. In many tribes, the various parts of the body are mapped out to symbolize in each case a prescribed type of classificatory relation, such as father, mother, sister's child, and so on. If an involuntary twitching occurs in a muscle in the part associated with the class of father, the person immediately abstracts himself from all surrounding interests and, letting his head droop forward, as I have seen, enters a condition either of receptivity or of free association. After a time, he becomes satisfied that such and such a person in the prescribed relationship will arrive before long. The information has "come" to him.[2]

To the Aborigines, there is nothing extraordinary about gaining information in these ways. Anyone can do so. But if he gets into difficulty or into doubt, for example, about the authenticity of a dream revelation or a presentiment, he can consult a specialist. For there are specialists; these are the medicine men, the clever men, the *karadji*, to use the term longest known to us. They are men of high degree.

The Personality of Medicine Men

Various questions arise concerning medicine men; what sort of persons are they? How are they selected, or how do they know that they are to be medicine men? What makes them what they are? What are their powers?

Let us consider the first question: What sort of persons are they?

A number of writers refer to the native doctor as an "impostor," "the greatest scamp of the tribe," or "as a rule the most cunning man in the tribe and a great humbug,"[3] These opinions, however, are based on superficial observation. When a native doctor sucks a magical bone out of a sick person's abdomen and shows it to those around and to the patient, he is not a mere charlatan, bluffing his fellows because he introduced and produced the bone at the psychological moment by sleight of hand. Nor is he just play-acting for effect when, having rubbed the affected part of his patient in the "correct" manner, he gathers an invisible something in his hands and, solemnly walking a few steps away, casts "it" into the air with a very decided jerk of the arms and opening of the hands. These are two of a number of traditional methods that he has learned, and in which he and all believe—

methods for extracting the ill from the patient and so giving the latter assurance (often visible) of his cure. The cause has been removed.

We should remember that if a medicine man himself becomes ill, he calls in a fellow practitioner to treat him in one of the accepted ways, although he knows all the professional methods (which we might call tricks). He also desires earnestly, like all other sick people, assurance that the cause of his pain or illness has been extracted and cast away, or that his wandering soul (if that be the diagnosis) has been caught and restored. The actions and chantings and production of "bones" and "stones" are but the outward expression and means of the doctor's personal victory over one or both of two factors: first, the malevolent activities of some person practicing sorcery on the sick man or woman; and second, the patient's willingness to remain ill or even to die. This latter must be counteracted and the will to be healthy and to live be restored.

Dr. F. E. Williams, referring to similar beliefs and practices among the Keraki of the Trans-Fly region of Papua, agrees that the doctor believes in his own power, although he realizes the trickery inherent in it. Dr. Williams, however, does not think that the Papuan doctor can be credited with sufficient insight to justify his methods as a means of restoring confidence in his patients.[4] But I can bear witness that there are Aboriginal medicine men who do justify and explain their procedure in just this way.[5]

To sum up: medicine men are not impostors. They practice their profession in the way that they and their fellow tribesfolk have inherited, and that they believe, and have found, to be effective. If a doctor's efforts fail, it means that he was summoned too late, or that the power of the distant sorcerer was too great, or that the patient had broken a very important taboo, or that the spirits of the "dead" would not be deprived of the company of the sick person's spirit; all of which finds an echo in our own experiences and attitudes.

It is reported, however, that an impostor may occasionally appear (like our charlatan) who claims to possess power and knowledge, hoping thereby to gain prestige or goods. But the shallowness of his claim is eventually seen through.[6] In any case, a medicine man must be able to maintain his prestige and "doctor personality" by success in his specialization or by convincing his tribesmen that his explanations of failures are satisfactory. Otherwise, faith in him will wane, and he will realize that he has lost his powers. He will recall that he has broken one or more of the taboos, on the observance of which the maintenance of his power depends. For example, a doctor must not drink hot water, must not be bitten by certain ants; must not be immersed in salt water, and must not eat certain foods. As the infringement of some of these may be accidental, the discredited practitioner has an honorable way out. In other cases, he can no longer practice because he has ceased to dream of the spirits of the dead. In some tribes, at least, a doctor who breaks the food taboos associated with his profession is discredited; indeed, it is only one with a very powerful personality who would dare risk his reputation and practice in this way.[7]

To practice a profession so "hedged about" with forms of "ritual" behavior that can be observed by all is at least some guarantee that the person concerned is genuine. Impostors are unlikely to appear except in a condition of tribal and cultural disintegration, when cunning persons might think there is an opportunity to gain some position of privilege. Moreover, unthinking and credulous white men sometimes encourage the medicine man to play on their desire for mystery. He recognizes what the white man hopes to hear, and desires to pay for, and lowering his voice to tones of secrecy, he relates satisfying tales of magic and mystery. But look at the glint of merriment in the old doctor's eyes, as he thinks to himself, "White man 'nother kind; white man fool."

Medicine Men, Outstanding Personalities

If the superficial observation of medicine men as scoundrels and impostors is not true, is it possible that it arises from the fact that these men are really clever, endowed with knowledge above the average and marked by strong personalities? Beneath the unkempt hair, above a naked body or one clothed in the white man's cast-offs, and in an immobile face shine shrewd, penetrating eyes—eyes that look you all the way through—the lenses of a mind that is photographing your very character and intentions. I have seen those eyes and felt that mind at work when I have sought knowledge that only the man of high degree could impart. I have known white people who almost feared the eyes of a *karadji,* so all-seeing, deep, and quiet did they seem. This clever man was definitely an outstanding person, a clear thinker, a man of decision, one who believed, and acted on the belief, that he possessed psychic power, the power to will others to have faith in themselves.

"You could always tell a medicine-man [*walemira*] by the intelligent look in his eyes," two Wiradjeri informants told R. M. Berndt, "and great ones were enveloped in a peculiar atmosphere which caused people to feel different."

The Reverend T. T. Webb, referring to the Murngin (northeast Arnhem Land), says that, speaking generally, the doctors are "not men of outstanding personality or of forcefulness of character," and Professor Warner, with reference to the same area, and Dr. W. E. Roth for northwest-central Queensland say that the doctor's personality was not different from that of any ordinary man, except that he was known to possess special magical powers.[8]

As a result of my own experience and of a close examination of reports on the subject, I am satisfied that medicine men are, generally speaking, persons of special knowledge, self-assurance, and initiative, and that association with them quickly reveals this fact. Nor is there anything mysterious or mystic about it:

1. They are men who have passed through a very striking ritual and experience of being "made" (to be described later); to face and to persist in this requires determination and courage.
2. They have been admitted to a special body of esoteric magic and psychic lore.
3. They have been taught, and also have learned by observation, much real insight into the working of the minds of their fellows.
4. They build up a store of information regarding the doings, especially the "sins" of omission and commission, of their fellows, which knowledge can be used, if necessary, as explanation of illnesses and accidents.[9]
5. They keep account, too, of the attitudes of their local group, clan, or tribe toward other groups, so that in case of "divining a murderer" at an inquest they can attribute the "crime" to a person or group whom their own group would be willing to suspect or blame.
6. They learn from their teachers and from observation the signs or symptoms of illnesses that can normally be cured, or from which the patient can be expected to recover, and in which their magical methods and faith healing are likely to be successful. Likewise, they can distinguish those that are likely to prove fatal; for those they must have satisfactory explanations, and their main task is to prepare the patient for death.
7. Those who claim power to predict or control natural phenomena possess a fund of knowledge concerning the

signs that mark changes in the weather, such as the seating ground, ants carrying their eggs upward for safety, the form of the clouds, variations in temperature, and suchlike. This enables them to act or speak with reasonable certainty.

8. In cases in which the clever men claim psychic powers and are expected to practice them, they have learned by instruction and practice how to do so; for example, how to interpret dreams, how to ascertain what is happening at a distance, or how to make those present "see" or believe that they, the "doctors," are moving through the air.
9. They are recognized by their tribe or community as possessing the power to outwit malign spirits and persons, to control the elements, to have foreknowledge of an enemy's approach, and to keep pestilence away from the camp.

I have not referred to what we might call the ordinary remedies for, and treatments of, ills and accidents. In many tribes, the old women attend to this, although in some the medicine man does so. Normally, however, his special power being occult, he is called in only when the illness is thought to be caused magically or animistically (by the actions of a malevolent person or spirit).

In the light of the foregoing facts, it is obvious that a medicine man, at least one who has not lost his *mana*, his power and prestige, must stand out in his community. He is superior in knowledge, in experience, and in psychic power, and this must be reflected in his attitude and general bearing, especially when he is confronted with the abnormal or unexpected. It is for this reason that he seems to be somewhat reserved except toward his fellow doctors, even though he is usually well liked.

Moreover, the medicine man's personality is not an individual phenomenon. Because of his "making" and training and deeds, a special social personality is ascribed to him by his fellows: He is essential to their social well-being and to the maintenance of satisfactory relations with the unseen—with the spirits of the dead and of the bush, with the rainbow serpent and the sky-being, and with sorcerers in strange places.

For all these reasons, we can say that the medicine man is a man of special, and often outstanding, personality.[10]

Medicine Men As Normal People

It has been maintained that medicine men are abnormal and neurotic.[11] At first sight, there might seem to be some justification for holding that there is something strange or queer about men who claim to have had their "insides" exchanged for spirit-insides, to carry quartz stones, bones, and spirit-snakes in their bodies—who claim to be able to converse with the dead, to travel invisibly through space, to visit the sky-land, and so on. But no observer records that Aboriginal medicine men, or sorcerers, are, apart from their occult powers and intellectual attainments, other than normal Aboriginal personalities. They live the ordinary family and social life and take part in the regular ritual and ceremonial life of their tribe like any other initiated men. As W. E. Roth said, and he was a physician who knew the Aborigines very well, "Beyond their occult powers [of curing and causing sickness], the doctors, except for certain articles which they kept about them, have nothing to distinguish them from the other individuals in the camp; they engage in similar pursuits, enjoy no extra rights; they marry and may themselves get sick or die through similar agencies."[12]

Among the Murngin, too, in spite of their occult experiences and powers, the medicine men live the ordinary life of all the tribesmen and are jovial and pleasant in their social relations. W. L. Warner saw no indications of psychopathic personality. On the contrary, the doctors are, psychologically and mentally, a very normal group.[13]

The point to be stressed is that while the medicine man is considered to possess great power and specially developed faculties, none of his power is regarded as extraordinary or abnormal. It is possessed and exercised against an accepted background of belief, and in some degree, though usually in a very slight degree, it is possessed by all. Everybody may have dream experiences of occult significance, though only the "trained" man may fully understand them. Everybody may have intimations of what is happening at a distance, although only the medicine man may be able to seek and obtain such knowledge by occult means. In many tribes, an individual's totem will bring him information and help in the waking or in the dreaming state; but it is usually only the medicine man who has an individual totem, or familiar, all to himself that assists him in various aspects of his profession. In some tribes, almost any person who cares to learn can work black magic, but it is only the doctor who can withdraw the effects of the magical rite from the victim.

The medicine man, for his part, simply possesses these and other faculties in a developed degree, the result of being gifted, of having passed through an experience of making, which gave him power and confidence, and of specializing and training. Moreover, he was first of all a fully initiated member of the tribe, disciplined by preparation for custodianship of tribal mysteries and indoctrinated with a respect for tribal sanctions and norms of life. Only after this did he pass through a ritual experience with its consequences of further power and knowledge. As such a man of high degree, he is a more complete exponent of normal life than those with less appreciation and understanding of the background of that life—a background that is mystical and psychic, magical and animistic. Moreover, unless a man were capable of such a high degree of normality, it is unlikely that he would receive the necessary training and insight from other doctors, and, in any case, he would not enjoy the confidence, respect, and prestige that are essential for a successful career. At least, there is no evidence of any person, except of this type, becoming a man of high degree. Aboriginal culture does not put any premium on the epileptic or abnormal of any sort. It is rather an expression of a world of order and normality, deriving from the long-past dreamtime of the culture-heroes, through the present, to the future.

Finally, emphasis should be placed on the fact that a medicine man's life is one of self-discipline, preceded by training, of social responsibility, and of contact with powerful forces or spiritual beings. He must work coolly and deliberately when his services are required, and not as some mental disturbance dictates or disposes. He does not seek the necessary knowledge or power through drug or violent dance but rather thorough quietness and receptivity, meditation and recollection, observation and inference, concentration and decision. His is a profession for which he has been duly prepared and trained. It is not a kink, though it is possible that sometimes a man may be misled into believing that he "was made" in some dream experience, but that alone will not accredit him. In the same way, we must distinguish among ourselves the well-trained and accredited psychotherapist and analyst from the amateur with a psychoanalytical or similar kink. It is the latter who is usually somewhat abnormal, and who seems unable to see through himself, or to realize that he should do so.

In other words, the real medicine man is a professional individual of special training whose personality, from the point of view of the community, reaches a high degree of normality.

How Selected or "Called"

An individual is selected or called to be a doctor in one of three ways:

1. The elders, and especially the medicine man, will have noticed that from the postulant's earliest years or from his youth he was gifted and had leanings toward the profession. He was a thoughtful child who liked being with the elders and the medicine men. He had probably shown a great interest in tribal lore and may even have had some psychic experiences. Indeed, his eyes may have revealed his fitness for the profession. Such early manifestation of fitness and association with medicine men while still a child seem to have been a necessary prerequisite in southeast Australia.[14] In the Wiradjeri tribe, for example, the lad's powers of interpretation were tested by the use of specially constructed sentences in conversation with him, and he was given intensive training in tribal mythology. He was also told about the simpler aspects of the profession and received his individual totem, or familiar.
2. Closely allied with this method of selection is that of inheritance of the position, or profession, of the medicine man. It is common in primitive and civilized societies for a father to desire that his son should succeed him in his social or professional position and to help him to do so. The sphere of magic and religion is no exception to that tendency. Of course, in the professional sphere descent alone is seldom enough, though nepotism has not been unknown there. Training, fitness, and acceptableness, however, are also necessary. And even among the Aborigines, a doctor's son has to have shown leanings and efficiency before he was trained and admitted to esoteric knowledge; in other words, even he had to be selected or at least accepted.

The profession has been reported as hereditary, mostly patrilineal, in western New South Wales, the southeastern corner of Queensland, parts of Cape York Peninsula, Eyre's Peninsula (South Australia), and in the Gascoyne and Ashburton districts of Western Australia. The power of sorcery also tends to pass from father to son in northeast Arnhem Land. More complete information might show that this tendency is more widespread than we now know. This is probably true also of the custom of selection in childhood.[15]

3. The third method is an inner experience of being "called," or in some cases one that results from a desire to be called. An individual has a vision of the spirits of the dead or of other spirits. This may occur just as he is waking out of a sleep in good health or when recovering from some illness. Or it may be deliberately sought by sleeping in an isolated place, particularly near the grave of a medicine man or some other enchanted spot. But if the aspirant's vision is interpreted by a medicine man as showing that he is called, he is taught what further psychic experiences to expect, and eventually he is trained in the profession.

An examination of the three ways of being called, and what follows, reveals a number of common features.

1. The postulant must be selected or accepted by a number of members of the profession, whether in childhood or later.
2. He must pass through a special psychic experience, which is indeed his validation—his certificate.
3. This experience follows prescribed patterns in different regions and therefore must be prepared for by meditation and other discipline; indeed, in some cases, and probably in most, if not all, medicine men, the past masters of the craft, really perform a ritual around and on the postulant,

which is an enactment of this remarkable experience; but to him in his state of expectancy and in later interpretation, it may seem to be caused solely by spirits, though nonetheless objective for that.

4. The postulant has to be trained in his profession and to be entrusted with its esoteric lore.

The Making of Medicine Men: Taking the High Degree

At first sight, there is nothing stranger in anthropological literature and in fieldwork than the descriptions given by Aboriginal medicine men of the way in which they received their power. These seem so impossible and fantastic that we could be pardoned for dismissing them as mere inventions or as the results of nightmare. But a study of the distribution of these experiences and an examination of their patterns give pause for thought. For the striking fact is not so much the weirdness of the details as their similarity over wide regions of the continent and even in apparently widely separated regions. In other words, we are confronted by a prescribed pattern of ritual experience through which medicine men are made. The following is a brief summary and analysis of the rites, based on the survey presented in chapters 3 and 4.

Uncircumcision Regions

South of the Murray River, medicine men were made by a supernatural spirit, or by the spirits of the dead, in the bush or in the sky. The normal procedure was for the spirit to open the postulant's side and to insert in it such magical substances as quartz crystals with which his powers were henceforth connected. The incision was healed without leaving a mark. Usually, too, the postulant was taken up to the skyworld. Indeed, the operation might be performed on him there. In any case, he could henceforth visit the sky and converse with the ghosts and spirits who dwell there.

In southwestern New South Wales, other medicine men, or a cult-hero, performed the central rite in the making. An incision was not made in the postulant's body, but in spite of that an assistant totem (or familiar) and magical substances such as quartz crystals and mysterious cord were pressed or rubbed and "sung" into him. He was also taken to the sky—this time on a doctor's magical cord. The experience seems to have been much the same in Gippsland (Victoria, Kurnai tribe) and on the north coast of New South Wales (Kumbaingeri tribe). In the latter district, after fasting and enduring privations for months, and even sleeping on a grave, the postulant was visited by the tribal Great Spirit or sky culture-hero, who put quartz crystals in his insides. The account for the Port Jackson tribe, farther south, suggests how this was done. The spirit of the deceased person seized the aspirant by the throat, made an incision, took out his intestines, which he "replaced," after which the wound closed up. Among the Yualai and Weilwan in northwestern New South Wales, the main operation was also performed by a spirit (or ghost) at a burial ground. One of them drove a yam-stick right through the postulant's head and placed in the hole a sacred stone-crystal, which is associated with the sky-hero. The power of the stone can also be obtained if it is swallowed or is rubbed into the postulant's or doctor's head.

In eastern Queensland, spirits of the dead, nature spirits, or the rainbow serpent is the source of power and plays an important part in the making, but, unfortunately, details of the ritual have not been recorded. Quartz crystals and a magical cord are signs and means of the medicine man's power and, in some parts at least, were carried in his insides, where they were put during the making.

Thus, in eastern Australia, magical substances and

"agents" were inserted into the postulant through an abdominal incision, or were rubbed or pressed and sung into his body and limbs, or the quartz might be inserted in a hole made through his head. The operators were the spirits of the dead, the sky culture-hero, or other supernatural spirits or medicine men. In some cases one of the last-named acted the part of the sky-hero. The operation or some significant part of the ritual was performed at a burial place. The purpose of this was not primarily to terrify and test the postulant, but to bring him into association with the spirits of the dead, whom in the future he would be able to see, consult, and summon to his aid. The ritual bestows powers to pass through the confines of death. But the central experience is usually interpreted or described as a trance, not a "death," whereas in the circumcision regions it is frequently referred to as the latter.

The interesting point, however, is that the same pattern of experience forms the central feature of the ritual of making medicine men right across South Australia, into the Great Victoria Desert of Western Australia, and north through Central Australia to the southwest corner of the Gulf of Carpentaria, as well as in some parts of the far northwest of the continent.

Circumcision Regions

Among the Dieri, near Lake Eyre, a spirit makes an incision in the postulant's abdomen and inserts a spirit-snake, his future familiar. The postulant also visits the sky by means of a hair-cord. In the neighboring Piladapa tribe, a spirit drives a "pointing-stick" into the back of the postulant's head, but the latter recovers and receives power and quartz from the spirit. Included in his power is that of extracting a person's "insides."

In western South Australia, the postulant is put in a waterhole, where a mythical snake swallows him but later ejects him in the form of a baby onto a supposedly unknown place. After a long search, he is found by the doctors and is restored to a man's size by being sung in the midst of a circle of fires. After a period of seclusion and converse with spirits, he is red-ochred and treated as a corpse. Then the head doctor ritually breaks his neck, wrists, and other joints by marking them with a magic stone (australite). Into each mark or cut, and also into his stomach, the doctor inserts *maban* life-giving shell, after which the postulant is sung and revives, now full of power.

The description of the operation in the Mandjindja tribe, Warburon Ranges, Western Australia, adds the detail that two totemic spirits or heroes "kill" the postulant, cut him open from his neck to his groin, take out all his insides, and insert magical substances (*mabain*). They also take out his shoulder and thigh bone and insert mabain before drying and putting them back. They treat the frontal bone in the same way and also cut around the ankles and stuff mabain into those parts.

In Central and North-central Australia, a similar experience must be endured. Spirits of the "eternal dreamtime" or spirits of the dead kill the postulant and through an abdominal incision remove his insides and substitute new ones together with some magical substances. If medicine men are the operators, the method is similar to that employed in the Wiradjeri and neighboring tribes of western New South Wales. Crystals, extracted from their own bodies, are pressed and scored and "jerked" into the postulant's body. He is also given crystals in his food and drink. In addition, a hole is pierced in his tongue.

This ritual is interpreted by the members of the profession as a "death," during which the postulant is operated upon and receives additions to his insides, and after which he is restored to life.

Light is thrown upon this by a Nyul-Nyul informant in

northwest Australia, who apparently did not wish me to think that the postulants actually had their abdomens incised and cleaned out, and their old, or else new, insides and magical substances inserted, as other informants had assured me. He said this did not happen, but that the operator put a small snake and shell into the postulant while he was asleep.

Information for northwestern Australia is meager, but it is of interest because, first, in both the Lagrange and Forrest River districts, the magical substances on which the doctor's power depends are called *maban,* the term used across the desert at the Warburton Ranges and down to Ooldea. Second, in these two districts, and in both East and North Kimberley generally, the medicine man is made by, or receives his power from, the rainbow serpent, or else a water snake, which can also be seen in the sky. And third, in the Kimberley districts, as in the Warburton-Ooldea districts, pearl-shell, an important magical possession, is associated with a mythical water snake, who, in some accounts, is definitely the rainbow. It comes to the Great Victoria Desert region from the Kimberley coastal tribes.

At Lagrange and in East Kimberley, this mythical snake makes the doctor, killing him being the first step in the process. In the Northern Kimberley at Forrest River, an old doctor takes the postulant, reduced to the size of a baby, to the sky either on a cord or on the rainbow, which serves as a rope. Reaching the sky, he throws him onto the sky-land, thus killing him. He then inserts in him *maban* (quartz crystals) and little rainbow snakes, which he can obtain in a waterhole at the foot of the rainbow. Bringing the postulant back to earth, he inserts more *maban* into him through his navel, after which he wakes him up with a magical stone. The new doctor then learns how to use pearl-shell and other *maban,* and how to go to the sky and to see the spirits of the dead.

This association of the making with a water or rainbow

snake and pearl-shell definitely connects the ritual in the Kimberleys with that in the Warburton-Ooldea region. The insertion of magical substances is, of course, an almost universal feature of the ritual, but going to the sky-world both as part of, and as a result of, being made, which is characteristic of East and North Kimberley, distinguishes it from the great central regions of the continent, though linking it with the southeastern region. In the Kimberleys, the sky-world holds in Aboriginal belief almost the same importance as in southeast Australia. Great culture-heroes live up there, and so do the dead in some districts, as in East Kimberley, for the doctor can visit them by going up on a string. But at the same time, there are spirit-homes on earth, not only for pre-existent spirits, but also for those awaiting rebirth.

In Arnhem Land we pass to a slightly different world—one in which sorcerers practice soul stealing.[16] We do not know how these sorcerers are made, but there are medicine men in the region, endowed with the usual curative, divining, clairvoyant, and thought-reading powers, and also with some control over the rain-making totemic python.

The main objective of their making in northeast Arnhem Land is to obtain familiars, who seem to be spirit-children with some birdlike characteristics. The aspirant to the profession must experience a vision of such familiars coming to and residing with him. Moreover, other doctors, and only doctors, can see these spirit-helpers. They must vouch that the new medicine man has gained some, usually two, of them. Ordinary people are convinced by hearing their clicking sounds—a kind of beating of wings against the doctor's shoulders.

Sometimes, as in far western Queensland, the vision may include the unpleasant experience of being half-stunned and having pointed objects thrust into one's body, and of being thrown into a waterhole and dragged out when almost drowned, after which the magical objects are extracted, and the aspirant feels better again. This is followed by a visit to a cave of ghosts, familiars, and a totem python. Some experiences of this type may be a feature of all making that are seldom divulged.

Other medicine men play an important part in the making and training of new practitioners in this region. But available information suggests that the gaining of the prescribed vision is essential. Anointing the body with a special preparation, sleeping in a solitary place, avoiding certain foods, and, of course, accepting in earnest faith the tribal beliefs regarding spirit-familiars are means to this end.

The Kakadu postulant (Arnhem Land) came into sacramental relation with a rainbow snake by being rubbed with, and drinking, some of the blood of its earthly snake representative. Afterward, with the help of this rainbow snake or one of its small earthly representatives, the doctor was able to rescue stolen souls.

The only other region for which any worthwhile information is available is far western Queensland. There, doctors are made by nature spirits who were probably ghosts to begin with, or by a water snake. The method seems to amount to a killing of the aspirant by "pointing" and projecting magical substances into his body. These are later removed. The individual has sought this experience by fasting and seclusion, and it seems certain that medicine men play a part in the trance experience. Indeed, if the trance does not come, the Maitakudi aspirant can be made by doctors of the Goa tribe. They kill him, throw him into a waterhole for four days, and then take him out and dry him in a ring of fires, so making him all right. In other words, he passes through a prescribed ritual, in which a water snake figures. The killing is apparently effected by pointing. We can be sure that only part of the making has been revealed.

To sum up the available evidence for South Australia, the neighboring area of Western Australia, the Northern Territory, far west Queensland, and the Kimberleys, the making of medicine men occurs by means of a transition rite that conforms to a traditional and significant pattern:

1. The postulant, who, of course, has been approved and accepted as a candidate, is killed, usually by being pointed with a magical death-bone; in the southwestern part of this large region, however, death comes through being swallowed by a great mythical water snake, which, like the rainbow, can reach the sky. The killing and the swallowing are interpreted as a death by the doctors and by the members of the postulant's group. The latter mourn for him, and an old man or the doctors search for his body.[17]
2. Operations are performed on the ritual "corpse." The abdominal incision is perhaps the most striking, but the temporary removal of the frontal bone and thigh bones should not be overlooked. Magical additions are made to the insides, head, thigh bones, and ankles and other joints.

   Some descriptions refer to magical pressing and scoring of the body, head, and limbs. Obviously, this is what actually occurs, even when major operations are described. The latter probably represent an esoteric interpretation. Moreover, the accounts of making by medicine men in the western South Australian and Kaitish and Waramunga tribes show that the initiating doctors do perform such major "operations" in ritual form.

   An important feature of the operation is the cleaning of the bones, the replacement of the insides with new ones, and the addition of magical substances and agents: quartz or pearl-shell, spirit-snakes, or other familiars.

3. Finally, the "dead" person is restored to life—a man of power.
4. During the making and afterward, the postulant is brought into contact with spirits and heroes of totemic significance, the spirits of the dead. The place of making is not a burial place. With the exception of the Dieri, the Binbinga, and the Mara tribes, in the east of the region, and some Kimberley tribes in the northwest, the doctors do not go to the sky. Those in the southeast of the continent do visit this world above, because it is the abode of the great cult-heroes and of the spirits of the dead. Incidentally, their place of making is usually at least partly associated with a burial ground.

Two explanations can be given of this remarkable fourfold experience. According to the first, the postulant is so conditioned by instruction, by seclusion in suitable surroundings, and by fasting and ceremony that he goes into a trance and sees all the correct, the suggested, and the expected happenings materialize. According to the second, after the conditioning by instruction, psychological preparation, and bodily ordeal, the killing, surgical operations, and restoration might, and in some cases do, occur in ritual manner, medicine men acting the roles of the great totemic spirits (or in the Mara tribe, of the sky-spirits). This is in keeping with the great part played by totemic ritual in the life of these tribes. Moreover, there is no doubt that in southeast Australia also, medicine men acted the role of the sky-hero (Baiame, for example). The Wiradjeri and other accounts make this clear.

An interesting feature of the ritual operation is that in southeast Australia it is usually referred to as a trance experience, and this is implied for northeast Arnhem Land, whereas in the other regions, it is almost always referred to as a death, or "being killed," the postulant being mourned for as one dead. Present information suggests a correlation of the emphasis on trance in southeast Australia with a greater development there than elsewhere of psychic practices, such as hypnotism, materialization, and thought transference. This seems to be the case also in northeast Arnhem Land. Further inquiry, however, in other regions may show that they are not exceptional in this regard.

A note. Another possible correlation, perhaps connected with this, is worth notice and further inquiry. The regions in which the making is referred to as a death belong almost wholly to the great fan-shaped circumcision-subincision area extending from the Kimberleys to the Roper River and far western Queensland, down to Spencer's Gulf, along the Great Australian Bight, and up to the Ninety-Mile Beach, south of Broome. In the initiation ceremonies in this area, circumcision is the main symbolic act of ritual death. Indeed, to initiate is to kill, signifying circumcision in particular, and in some parts of the area the foreskin is disposed of according to the "burial" practice of the tribes concerned. Subincision expresses sympathy and also ritual solidarity, and in one large region at least signifies "paying with a life."

On the other hand, the regions in which the most striking features of the making of medicine men are described as a trance or other psychic experience, and not referred to as death or being killed, are the uncircumcision regions. In most, if not all, of eastern Australia, initiation into tribal membership is termed "putting, or going, through the rule." In this region, too, medicine men are the masters of the secret life and take the leading part in initiation, whereas in the circumcision regions, the headmen of the cult-totemic life, who are not necessarily medicine men, fulfill both these roles, and the main revelations consist of rites, myths, and symbols of the totemic heroes of the "eternal dreamtime."

In other words, where tribal initiation includes circumcision and subincision, and the headmen of the totemic cult-lodges are masters of the ritual, the making of medicine men is commonly referred to as a killing or death; whereas in the uncircumcision regions, where the clever men are the masters, and the emphasis is on going through the rule and, incidentally, being brought into relationship with the sky-world and its cult-hero, the crucial experience of the doctor-postulant is thought of as a trance or psychic experience.

Northeast Arnhem Land tribes, however, whose rites for the making of medicine men are referred to explicitly in psychic terms, as a vision or dream, practice circumcision and so are an exception to the above generalization. But like a number of other tribes on the margin of the circumcision area, they do not practice subincision, or else do not make it compulsory. The distribution of these rites suggests that there has been and is a time lag between the adoption of the two, and that a tribe that possesses only the former has done so for a comparatively short time. If so, this would mean that the significance of the circumcision rite has not yet affected the interpretation of the ritual of making in northeast Arnhem Land.

Likewise, the Piladapa and Ngaduri of South Australia, who are in the circumcision area but do not practice subincision, and the Dieri, who are just within the subincision boundary, belong, according to the available accounts, to the strongly developed psychic southeast region (see chapter 4). Whether or not a longer experience of the myths and rituals of circumcision and subincision would have modified the interpretation of the medicine man making in these tribes cannot now be determined.

The above is merely a suggestion, which must be examined more thoroughly. In particular, a study should be made, as soon as possible, of medicine men and their powers in those parts of the circumcision-subincision area where the opportunity still remains.

Distribution of Abdominal Operation

A survey of the continent reveals that the abdominal operation for the purpose of inserting magical paraphernalia or new insides as part of a ritual of death and restoration is recorded for the southeast (Victoria and Port Jackson), a large region covering northern and western South Australia, the neighboring area of Western Australia, Central and North-central Australia, and Dampier Land in the far northwest. In some cases, incisions are made in other parts of the body for the same purpose.

Closely related to this, and as part of a similar death and restoration rite, is the insertion of magical paraphernalia into the postulant's abdomen, head, and limbs without definite mention of abdominal or other incisions—the latter being the esoteric interpretation of the former. This is recorded from western New South Wales, far western Queensland, and the Kimberley Division (northwestern Australia).

Mummification Pattern of Ritual

Since the making of medicine men is a transition rite, it is not surprising to find it follows a death and a restoration-to-life pattern, modeled on the most decisive of all human experiences—death itself. As I have pointed out elsewhere,[18] if the ritual concerned with an actual corpse consisted of making an abdominal and other incisions; removing, cleaning, and replacing the internal organs; adding magical or life-giving substances; closing the incisions; and a ritual "raising" of the body to life, we would call the process one of mummification. We would be all the more justified in doing this since the postulant's body is usually specially prepared, for example, by being anointed with red ochre and in some cases by being steeped in water for a period and then dried amid fires, and since as a result of the ritual the person is like a member of the ghostly world. He can visit and converse with the departed and traverse in body and mind both space and time without hindrance. In other words, his body is believed to become what the Egyptians said the ritually mummified corpse had become, a Zed, a living body.

But whence came this ritual into Australia? Did it come with the diffusion of the profession of medicine men and of certain forms of magic into the continent? This is possible, for esoteric rites do spread from people to people. Or was it built up in Australia on the basis of an actual burial rite that was performed there, whether introduced or evolved locally?

No definite answer can be given, but it is suggestive that in eastern Australia from Cape York Peninsula down eastern Queensland and the Darling River to the mouth of the River Murray and parts of Victoria, a form of mummification burial ritual was practiced, though usually only in the case of important men and doctors. This ritual varies slightly along its 3,200 kilometers of distribution, but it follows a general pattern:

1. The preparation of the body by removing the intestines and stomach temporarily or altogether through an abdominal incision, and sometimes by removing the outer skin; in one north Queensland rite, incisions are also made in the shoulders and lungs, and filled with stones. The body is then bound up and usually painted and dried in the sun or over a fire.
2. It is next made up into a bundle, the "mummy," which is carried around by the mourners until their grief is assuaged or revenge has been taken.
3. It is finally disposed of by interment, cremation, or exposure.[19]

There seems little or no reason for doubting that this ritual was introduced into Australia by way of the Torres Straits Islands, where a type of mummification was practiced.[20] It is, therefore, possible, if not probable, that the ritual for the making of medicine men was based on it and diffused right across Australia. It is unfortunate that we have no information regarding this ritual for north and east Queensland, but whatever it was there, the spread of the ritual of which we have knowledge could have been from the Darling River region to the Cooper's Creek region, and so to Central and northern and northwestern Australia. The Molonga ceremony was diffused in those directions and so, too, was the matrilineal dual organization, as far as it went.[21] In any case, a secret ritual of this type spreads very much more quickly and widely than does a new burial ritual; for the latter is public and may run counter to current attitudes and beliefs. The Australian origin of the ritual of making, however, is only conjecture, and, as already suggested, it may have been introduced. If so, this may have been either from the northwest or from the northeast.

Medicine Men Making, A Pre-enactment of Magical Killing

One important aspect of the ritual of making medicine men is that in most areas the ritual killing and operation are a pre-enactment of the magical killing that occurs in those areas and that the postulant, if he chooses to practice sorcery, will later be able to perform. In the first place, in every region the doctor's power depends partly on magical substances, such as quartz, shells, stones, bones, and snakes, which are put into him during the ritual. But any of those objects, magically projected by him into another person, may be agents of sickness and death as well as of life. In his case, however, he is given the power to control them within his own body and to make them pass in or out at will. They are to him sources of power not of death.

In the second place, in many of the rites the postulant is killed by being pointed with a death-bone or by having magical objects projected into him. He is later revived by having these things withdrawn by the methods he will later use.[22]

In the third place, the ritual abdominal incision can be correlated with the practice of taking the kidney or caul-fat in southeast Australia and parts of northwest Australia, and with *kadaitja* in Central Australia and western South Australia. In kadaitja, a medicine man heals the wound made by a magical spearing after having inserted in the victim's insides something of magical power, such as a spirit-snake. No mark is left. In both these practices the victim revives and feels quite well but in about three days sickens and dies.[23]

Another example of this ritual experience of a magical death as a pre-enactment of what the postulant can later do comes from Central Australia. In one method of making, the spirits throw an invisible lance, which pierces the postulant's neck from behind, making a large hole and coming out through the mouth. A second lance pierces his head from ear to ear. Sometimes magical stones are thrown so as to penetrate the head in this way. Incidentally, medicine men have a large hole pierced in their tongue. And away to the southwest in the Great Victoria Desert, a cause of death is to choke the victim by pushing an invisible stick through his collarbone, neck, and tongue, and by inserting little stones and arm blood in his ears.

These facts illustrate the general principle that ritual is a pre-enactment of some experience or condition that is desired for the future. The doctor must pass through the experience of being magically killed and raised before he can either kill others or raise, that is, cure, them. The ritual is also a reenactment of what has occurred in the past, generally to a cult-hero. If this is not always clear, at least supernatural beings, dreamtime or sky heroes, or spirits of the dead are regarded as the operators, that is, the masters of the craft. They are the doctors, who control magic and death.

Medicine Man's Power Supernatural

Training in his craft is necessary for the medicine man, but that only teaches him how to prepare to receive, and how to use, the power to which time, space, matter, and death are subject. This power exists because the sky culture-heroes and the eternal dreamtime ancestors and heroes have shown that they possess it. The object of the ritual is to receive it from the heroes, from the historic source of the cult and through an unbroken channel. This is done by being magically and ritually treated by them, either in trance and vision, or by doctors representing them, or in both ways. So in the southeast, the postulants are taken to Baiame in the sky or in a prepared spot, or here, too, and also in the north and far northwest, they go to the sky. In the central regions they are operated on by dreamtime heroes, and in southeast and far western Queensland, in the Murray River district in western South Australia, in the Kimberleys, and in parts of Arnhem Land, they receive power from the rainbow, or other water serpent, who is usually connected with the sky.

Moreover, the power is received in symbolic and indeed sacramental forms that come from the heroic beings. In eastern Australia, and in the far northwest, quartz is such a symbol; it is living and is connected with the sky-world and with the rainbow, at the foot of which it may be obtained.

In Central and North-central Australia, quartz crystals are also the doctor's most potent medium, but what might be called their sacramental and theological nature has not been described for us.

In the western part of the continent, pearl-shell is the most important medium of power. Like quartz, it is connected with the rainbow serpent; and in both cases one reason might well lie in their reproduction of the colors of the rainbow, which might seem to be magical. In any case, the rainbow connects them both with the sky.

Spirit-snakes and other familiars of totemic and dreamtime associations are also sacramental links with the world of heroes and creative power.

This world is believed to be the source of life in man and nature, and all fully initiated men are links with it. But only men of high degree, men who in their special initiation have been admitted to this world in the sky and on earth—only those men can exercise that power to prevent death, to restore life, to recapture the soul, to converse with the dead, and to understand in some real measure the workings of the human mind.

Notes

1. A. P. Elkin, *The Australian Aborigines: How to Understand Them*, 5th edition (Sydney: Angus & Robertson, 1974), chapter 8.
2. A. P. Elkin, "Notes on the Psychic Life of the Australian Aborigines," *Mankind* 2, no. 3 (1937): 50.
3. G. Taplin, "The Narrinyeri" in J. D. Woods, *The Native Tribes of South Australia* (Adelaide: E. S. Wigg, 1879), p. 46. C. Lumholz, *Among Cannibals* (London: M. L. Hutchinson, 1889), p. 183. C. Strehlow, *Die Aranda—und Loritja—Stamme*, part 4, p. 42. Strehlow says the "doctors" in general are the greatest swindlers and conjurers, who, by means of their deceits and frauds, are able to keep the people in dependence on them. W. E. Roth, *Ethnological Studies among the North-West-Central Queensland Aborigines* (Brisbane: Government Printer, 1897). When Roth says the doctors do not trust one another and "in reality are a 'bad lot,'" he is referring to their practice of sorcery, and their keeping alive and potent the belief in the death-bone. See also A. W. Howitt, *The Native Tribes of South-East Australia* (London: Macmillan, 1904), p. 356.
4. F. E. Williams, *Papuans of the Trans-Fly* (Oxford: Oxford University Press, 1936), p. 354.
5. I think particularly of a *karadji* of the Kattang tribe, Port Stephens District, New South Wales, who maintained that what made the patient better was his faith in himself. If the karadji told him to get up next morning after the "treatment" and he did so, he would be cured; otherwise he would pine away. Elkin, "Notes on the Psychic Life," p. 52.
6. A. P. Elkin, Field Notes. Also W. E. Roth, *Superstition, Magic and Medicine*, North Queensland Ethnography Bulletin no. 5, 1903, p. 31. C. C. Greenway, "Australian Language and Traditions," *Journal of the Royal Anthropological In-*

stitute 7:243. P. Kaberry, *Aboriginal Woman, Sacred and Profane* (London: George Routledge, 1939), p. 251.

7. For example, H. Basedow, *The Australian Aboriginal* (Adelaide: F. W. Preece, 1925), p. 180: "In the Central Australian tribes a medicine-man should not eat of kangaroo which has been feeding upon new green grass; if he does, some of his mystic powers will leak out of his body, and he will immediately drop in the estimation of his tribal admirers. If the offence is repeated a number of times, he is discredited entirely. . . . There are, of course, a great number of restrictions which the conscientious practitioner observes most punctiliously." See also C. Strehlow, pp. 39, 42. B. Spencer and F. J. Gillen, *Native Tribes of Central Australia* (London: Macmillan, 1899), p. 525. The medicine man must not eat fat or warm meat, nor inhale smoke from burning bones, nor be bitten by a "bull-dog" ant. B. Spencer and F. J. Gillen, *Northern Tribes of Central Australia* (London: Macmillan, 1904), pp. 481, 485. Drinking anything hot is forbidden. In the Warramunga, numerous food restrictions must be observed by a doctor until he is old, and he must drink only a moderate amount of water. See W. L. Warner, *A Black Civilization, A Social Study of an Australian Tribe* (New York: Harper, 1937), pp. 217–18, for saltwater taboo. Warner does not think that the Murngin doctors observed any food taboos except during their making and training. Ibid. p. 216.
8. T. T. Webb, "The Making of a Marrngit," *Oceania* 6, no. 3:337. Warner, *Black Civilization*, p. 210. Roth, *Ethnological Studies*, pp. 153–54.
9. Roth, *Superstition, Magic*, p. 154, referring to northwest-central Queensland, says that whenever a large number of natives are in the camp, doctor is believed to keep his eyes and ears well open, and not to go to sleep at night. He thus gleans heaps of information and also often learns who possesses a death-bone and even the name of the person "pointed."
10. The following references bear on the above discussion. Kaberry, *Aboriginal Woman*, p. 252. R. M. and C. H. Berndt, "A Preliminary Report of Field-Work in the Ooldea Region," *Oceania* 14, no. 1:58–61. R. M. and C. H. Berndt, unpublished report on the Wiradjeri. Warner, *Black Civilization*, pp. 198, 230–32. W. E. Harney, personal correspondence. Basedow, *Australian Aboriginal*, p. 179. Spencer and Gillen, *Native Tribes*, p. 522, say that the medicine men "have considerable influence in the tribe." W. Ridley, *Kamilaroi and Other Australian Languages* (Sydney, 1875, 2nd edition), p. 158. "The Kuradyis exercise a strong spell over the minds of their people." This spell still exists among the old people in 1944, as my inquiries (September 1944) have shown. J. Dawson, *Australian Aborigines, The Language and Customs of Several Tribes* (Melbourne: G. Robertson, 1881), p. 56; referring to tribes in southwestern Victoria, Dawson says that great confidence was reposed in the skill of the tribal doctor, and not without reason, for he generally prescribed sensible remedies. When these failed, he had resource to supernatural means of vari-

ous artifices. W. L. Sharp, "Ritual Life and Economics of the Yir-Yoront," *Oceania* 5, no. 1:36, says that reputed ability in killing or curing adds to an individual's prestige.

11. P. Radin, *Primitive Religion: Its Nature and Origin* (London: Dover, 1937), pp. 131–32. Radin says that Aranda medicine men are of neurotic epileptoid type.
12. Roth, *Ethnological Studies*, pp. 153–54.
13. Warner, *Black Civilization*, p. 210. Webb, "Making of a Marrngit," p. 337. R. M. and C. H. Berndt, "Preliminary Report," pp. 61–62.
14. This was so among the Wurundjeri (Victoria), Wiradjeri and associated tribes and the Yualai (New South Wales), and the Dieri (South Australia). It is also reported for the Aluridja tribes now at Ooldea in the same state.
15. See chapters 3 and 4. In some tribes of northwest-central Queensland, a magical object may be inserted in a novice when a child, to make him a medicine man. Roth, *Ethnological Studies*, p. 153, implies that selection while still a child was not the necessary or regular practice, as seems to have been the case in the Wiradjeri, New South Wales.
16. This is done either by letting out the heart-blood, the soul escaping with this blood, or by causing the victim to take a deep breath, which opens the heart and lets the soul escape through the mouth. See chapter 4.
17. A. P. Elkin, "Beliefs and Practices Connected with Death in North-eastern and Western South Australia," *Oceania* 7, no. 3:289–91. A human-hair girdle is put around the postulant before he is thrown to the water snake. In this part of the region, the final act of mourning is to throw a girdle made of the dead person's hair into one of the waters associated with this snake, who swallows it.
18. Elkin, *Australian Aborigines*, pp. 332–33, 354. A. P. Elkin "Primitive Medicine Men," *Medical Journal of Australia* (November 30, 1935), p. 756.
19. Ibid.
20. W. R. Dawson, "Mummification in Australia and in America," *Journal of the Royal Anthropological Institute* 58 (1928): 115–21. Ursula H. McConnel, "Mourning Ritual Among the Tribes of Cape York Peninsula," *Oceania* 7, no. 3:350. A. P. Elkin, "Ritual Distribution in Australia," *Oceania* 16, no. 1:1ff.
21. Howitt, *Native Tribes*, p. 330. Roth, *Ethnological Studies*, pp. 117–18. B. Spencer and F. J. Gillen, *Wanderings in Wild Australia*, vol. 1 (London: Macmillan, 1928), pp. 237–38. Elkin, Field Notes. I saw parts of the Molonga ceremony at Horseshoe Bend (Aranda tribe) in 1930. A survey of the distribution of the matrilineal dual organization (Queensland, south of the Gulf of Carpentaria; western New South Wales and Victoria; and eastern South Australia to Eyre's Peninsula, except the Lower Murray) and an examination of the mythology shows that this cultural trait was diffused in a southern and southwestern direction. See A. R. Radcliffe-Brown, *Social Organization of Aus-*

tralian Tribes, Oceania Monograph, no. 1, pp. 48–70, and map, p. 10. A. P. Elkin, "The Social Organization of South Australian Tribes," *Oceania* 2, no. 1:52–53.

22. Chapters 3 and 4.
23. For kadaitja, see Elkin, *Australian Aborigines,* pp. 313–15, Spencer and Gillen, *Native Tribes,* pp. 476–85. For fat-taking, see Elkin, *Australian Aborigines,* pp. 308–10, 334–35; and chapters 3 and 4.

CHAPTER 2

The Powers of Medicine Men

The powers of medicine men are supernormal, usually supersensory, and are derived from two sources: first, the cult-heroes of the craft—sky and totemic heroes, spirits and ghosts, who may be all one; second, the long line and hierarchy or order of medicine men, which leads back to these same heroes of the eternal dreamtime.

Some doctors are also leeches, diagnosing illness and applying tribal remedies, and to this day faith in their treatment is great. Their special curative function, however, goes beyond this. They are concerned with the animistic, the magical, and the superordinary causes of illness and death. These cases are not abnormal to the Aborigines, even though they are to us. They are normal, but in a sphere of the normal with which only a class of specialists can deal—men with special training and power.

Medicine men's powers enable them to do many supernormal things, but they are all psychical in character. Healing or killing (by sorcery), "divining" a murderer, practicing hypnotism, telepathy, telesthesia, and clairvoyance, holding seances or visiting the sky—all these depend on the psychic training and faculties of the medicine man and the induction of the right state of receptivity (acceptivity, as it is called by Baudouin[1]) in the mind of the patient, victim, mourners, dreamers, or audience at a ceremony.

Sorcery and Its Cure

An Explanation of Illness and Death

Sorcery, or black magic, provides the explanation of illnesses, pains, and deaths, the causes of which are not known or obvious. The explanation is personal or spiritistic. Someone or some spiritual powers performed black magic because ill-disposed to the victim, or because the latter broke some taboo. But being personal or animistic, it can be dealt with by the specialist, and either health can be restored to the individual or at least equilibrium can be regained by the group. Not to know the causes of illness and death of tribesmen, by which the solidarity and efficiency of the community are weakened, is a disturbing factor in psychological and social life, but to have an accepted explanation and to have acted on that explanation enables the community to readjust itself to events and go about its business.

Thus the bone, the quartz or other stone, or the bad blood is magically extracted, or the wandering soul is brought back, and all is well. Or if this cannot be done, the victim and his group are prepared for the death of the former, and attention is paid to the inquest and revenge.

In many tribes, any person may learn to work some forms of black magic; and in many, too, medicine men can work serious and death-dealing forms of it, though such men seldom do so. In a few tribes only are there any self-confessed sorcerers. This last is a risky profession, even though its members may gather some sense of pride from their prowess. Sometimes illness is attributed to them, even though they have not acted at all. Possibly they eventually believe that they did exercise malign power, even in those cases.

Pointing and Other Forms of Sorcery

The important aspect of the potent forms of sorcery is that, whatever the implement used (pointing bone or other), and whatever the traditional form of words or spell employed, the performer must concentrate his thoughts on the victim; he must visualize him and transmit to him the thought of illness or death, of having a "bone" in his insides, or of having his kidney fat stolen. Using the traditional mechanism in the prescribed way and saying the prescribed words in a quiet undertone help in this concentration and direction of the mind. But this is not enough. The rite is not mechanical and external. It is psychic. This explains why the performer must observe taboos on his conduct and prepare himself for his task.

Whether the unseen and distant magical rite alone causes illness and death has yet to be proved, but certainly once the intended victim knows that he has been pointed, he will sicken and die, unless cured by a medicine man. Generally, however, in my opinion, the belief that one has been pointed follows the oncoming of certain pains and illnesses. The patient may, in a dream, see himself being pointed and sung, no doubt the result of pondering on his condition. In any case, it provides the explanation and also a possibility of recovery.

Doctor and Patient

In diagnosis and treatment, the doctor, working against a common background of faith, and of accepted explanation and methods, directs his efforts to dealing with the unseen animistic and psychic causes of illness and death. His paraphernalia of quartz and other stones, shell, spirit-snakes and other familiars are all aids to himself and his patient. Concentrating on his task, softly changing his words of power, rubbing, sucking, and all the rest of it are the sacramental forms—the means by which the doctor exercises his magical and psychic power and extracts and casts away the badness.

The patient, for his part, is in a condition of receptivity, of high suggestibility, and is ready to realize the idea suggested by the doctor's actions, by the objects he exhibits, and by his attitude of authority and certainty: the idea, namely, that the immediate cause of the illness has been removed, and that therefore he can recover. If, however, the doctor assures him and his people that he (the doctor) cannot extract the cause, or cannot bring back the wandering soul, then the patient likewise accepts the suggestion—the suggestion of death. He "turns his face to the wall," thinks of the spirits of the departed, and before long joins them.

The following is the treatment of a man who believes himself pointed, and who, as a result, has a dream or vision confirming this. The medicine man shows the patient a bunch of feathers and then goes to the door of the patient's wurley, where he sits quietly gazing at the sick man's body. Presently he closes his eyes, as though shutting out an evil vision, and professes to speak with the patient's departed relatives. He then gives the patient two feathers and tells him to place them in front of his eyes and look through them at his, the doctor's, body. The patient is startled, because the doctor's body appears to be transparent. When asked what he sees, he says to the medicine man: "It seems that your flesh has disappeared, and that I am able to see your spirit-man."

The doctor then removes the feathers from the sick man's eyes and at the same time enjoins him to close his eyes. He emphasizes his power to give or take life but adds that he is having a difficult time because the sick man's departed relations want him to join them in the spirit world. Indeed, they are beside him now, pleading with the doctor in the spirit-language to allow the patient to pass over. Then, placing two feathers in front of his own eyes, the doctor looks through them into the body of the patient and with a few "passes" of his hand across the latter, produces a broken stick. He explains that the sick man's departed relatives have prevented him from extracting the whole stick, and that therefore nothing more can be done.

The medicine man sits quietly watching the patient. He cries and bids the latter farewell. Then the relatives and friends come in and tell the sick man that he must resign himself to the wishes of the departed ones. "So he turns to the west and allows his spirit to take flight." He dies by suggestion, as Aborigines can, and as so many do.[2]

In this case, we see all the conditions present and methods used, which are considered essential for making suggestion effective. The patient is in an "acceptive" condition, with voluntary effort annulled and the associative process in abeyance. He is convinced that he has been pointed and believes absolutely that his living or dying depends solely on the medicine man.

The latter, on this basis, adopts an almost hypnotic attitude and approach, so that the patient becomes even more acceptive to his idea. He gazes at him silently, after drawing attention to his presence by showing him the feather—a sign of magical power. He speaks to the spirits and so creates atmosphere and then gets the patient to gaze through the feathers at his, the doctor's, body and to see only the latter's "spirit-man."

The patient is now ready to receive the suggestion—in the case, death. Being told to close his eyes, he hears the doctor's quiet but authoritative voice, leading up to the suggestion that the spirits have prevented a cure because they want the patient to join them. And he does.

In cases of serious illness, especially if experience has shown that there is hope of recovery from the particular type of illness, the doctor's task is a much more vigorous one. The diagnosis may require much time and also consultation with fellow practitioners and with relatives of the patient. Of course, everyone is very solemn, and the conversation is subdued. But when the cause has been determined, the patient is supported in a half-sitting attitude, with the medicine man standing close by, gazing upon him most intently. Suddenly he goes some distance off and, looking fiercely at him, bends slightly forward and repeatedly jerks his arm outward at full length, with the hand outstretched, to project magical stones into the patient's body. Then, going rapidly and with characteristic high knee action from one end of the cleared space to the other, he repeats the movements with dramatic action. Finally, he comes to the patient and by much mysterious searching finds the magical material cause of the illness, sucks it out, and displays it to all around.[3]

There is no doubt that such an energetic and dramatic performance on his behalf must lift the patient's thoughts away from his trouble and prepare him for the suggested idea of recovery—the manifestation of the bone. It is just as clear that the medicine man must exercise much concentration of thought and throw himself, mind and body, into the performance, because he must extract the illness along with the magic bone or stone; he must convince the patient that he will recover, or else his own reputation will be lowered, or at least not enhanced. What is more, failure might prove that he has lost his magical power.

Thought Transference

I have suggested that the use of the pointing bone and other forms of protective magic imply a belief that a person can send his thought through space, and also his visualization of the condition he wishes to produce. But this demands much effort and concentration. Mrs. Verrall, the famous sensitive, said, "All who have tried to convey an idea by thought transference must be familiar with the sensation that after a special effort, the thought has been actually projected into space, leaving one fatigued and conscious of loss."[4]

An Aboriginal medicine man, a friend of mine, years before I read this, impressed on me what hard work and effort were entailed in putting one's thoughts into the mind of a person at a distance and causing the latter to act upon them. He assured me that he could do it and had done so.

A person who has this faculty can use it for good or ill. Thus, in the Lower Murray River region, the *ngathungi* is a very potent form of pointing bone. It consists of a stick to which is fastened an object that has been in contact with the victim, especially the remnant of a meal. The person who operates it, however, must be an expert. He must possess the power of concentration and of communicating without physical means or agency; he must also be a person with a good many years of training.

When using this magical implement, the operator takes it in his left hand and says very softly, "Shooh Ho! Let the breath leave thy body, O boy!" Then he chants a song of hate for an hour or more, after which he warms part of the ngathungi, concentrates his mind until he sees a picture of his victim, and then with all the emotion and energy he can summon, he whispers "Die!" He lies down for an hour, no doubt gathering fresh psychic strength, and then repeats this performance several times, each time whispering: "Let the life-breath leave thy body, O boy! Die!" In fact, he keeps the mental picture of his victim before him all night. Finally, in the early morning, he performs similarly but this time as close as possible to the victim, provided the latter is asleep.[5]

This performance shows that the ritual use of what might be called a contagious implement of magic does not automatically produce the desired result. The operator must not only use the appropriate object in the correct way and say the prescribed words. He must also throw himself into the rite, not vociferously, but through psychic concentration and direction. The belief in the certainty of the result is a good example of man's belief in the omnipotence of thought.[6] At least, he realizes that he must "see" the victim, visualize the desired result, and send his thought to attain it. Usually a pointing bone only symbolizes and helps to transmit the thought of death; ideally, it is a bone from a dead person. But in this case, in which contagious magic centers, the bone or other implement may also help the performer call up the picture of his victim.

Psychical research is now suggesting that the holding of an article that had been in the possession of, or in contact with, an absent person puts the "sensitive" en rapport with such subject, and then she (or he) can read the latter's mind.[7] It is not suggested that it enables such a sensitive to affect, or transfer thoughts to, the latter, but at least it does suggest that a sorcerer endowed with this supernormal faculty could be helped by the use of a "contagious" element.

While referring to the possible practice of telepathy among the Aborigines, mention might be made of the following type of occurrence, which I have observed. A native is asked to obtain some information from another native who is sitting down about a kilometer away. The former does not shout out to draw the other man's attention, as we would probably do. He just utters a quiet, fairly long-drawn note, and soon the distant man gets up and turns round. It hardly seems possible that the call could have been heard, but, of course, the Aborigines are probably accustomed and attuned to hear much quieter noises than we are. So there may be nothing mysterious about it.

Then, without the first man raising his voice or saying very much, and with the use of a few signs between the two men, the information is gathered. These two men have a background of experience and knowledge that enables them to dispense with much talking and noise.

All cases, however, are not as easy to explain as this. A researcher has recently obtained texts in the native language of the Lower Murray River people concerning their psychic life that are somewhat startling.[8]

Here is one case, given in free translation:

> When a man is down on the plain and I am on the hill, I look towards him while I am talking. He sees me and turns toward me. I say, "Do you hear?" I move my head from side to side glaring at him, and at last stare at him, and then, turning, I say, "Come on quickly." As I stare at him fixedly, I see him turn as he feels my stare. He then turns and looks about while I continue staring at him. So I say, "Walk this way, right along here, where I am sitting." Then he walks right up to me where I am sitting behind a bush. I draw him with my power (*miwi*). You do not see any hand-signs or hear any shouting. At last he comes up and nearly falls over me. I call out so that he will see me. He says: "You talked to me and I felt it. How did you talk so?" I explain, and he adds: "I felt your words while you were talking to me, and then I feel that you are there." I answer. "True, it was in that way that I talked to you, and you felt those words and also that power."[9]

Clever men in other tribes claim to be able to exert this power. It can also be used to divert sorcerers from their evil intention. I quote a free translation of a text from the same area:

> When the "clever man" sees the two sorcerers going out to practice *milin* (bruising), he gazes or concentrates in such a way as to make their nerves cold (dead). When you see a clever man, his small eyes and your eyes meet and hold each other. He holds the sorcerers in this way, when he talks to them. They "feel" (but do not hear) his words, because their nerves are deadened. He makes them walk away from him, by exerting the strong power in his nerves, which begin to twitch. The men, under the influence of his gaze, weaken, and become as if asleep, and so when he says, "Go on, you! Walk down to the camp," they go. He tells them further: "Don't get up with the intention of performing sorcery." So they lie down and get up in the morning good (i.e., rid of the idea of performing sorcery). And, concludes the clever man, "That is the way some of us talk."

This seems to be a case of hypnotic influence, although the men's minds (subconscious, probably) had first to be drawn to the clever man and put en rapport with him. His narrow eyes and his gaze, together with their belief that he would know the antisocial nature of what they proposed doing, would no doubt do the latter.

Clairvoyance and Mind Reading

Our medicine men not only claim to be able to influence people who are at a distance, that is, to practice telepathy, they also assert that they see or ascertain by invisible means what is happening at a distance and, in some cases, can tell what another person is thinking.

"Sometimes," said Willidjungo, a Murngin medicine man, to W. L. Warner, "I am sitting with a man and I look at his head and I can say to him, 'You think so and so.' The man says, 'How do you know that?' And I say, 'I can see inside your mind.'"[10]

One purpose of pressing or scoring magical substances (quartz, pearl-shell, etc.) into a postulant's forehead is to enable him to see into and through everything.[11]

Various methods are used for learning what is occurring at a distance. A usual method, or explanation, is that the medicine man sends his familiar (his assistant totem, spirit-dog, spirit-child, or whatever the form may be) to gather the information. While this is occurring, the man himself is in a state of receptivity, in sleep or trance. In modern phraseology, his "familiar spirit" would be the control, or on the other hand, the medicine man may be sensitive to thoughts of other people's minds. He is indeed able, once he can get en rapport with, or visualize, them, to ransack their minds—a process termed telesthesia and not confined to ransacking the mind as it is at the time of inquiry, but also as it was in the past.[12]

Related to this is the clever man's power (as I learned in 1944 in northwest New South Wales, from the Kamilaroi and other tribes) of seeing in quartz crystal and glasslike stones what people are, or have been, doing, especially if contrary to social standards. Possibly the clever man has heard something before reading the crystal.

In many tribes, especially in southeast Australia, medicine men "can fly" through space and see what is occurring elsewhere. They might produce magical cord or familiars and travel on or in them, or they might pass through the air without such accessories. Normally, however, their bodies do not take part in these journeys; only their spirits do. Indeed, their bodies are sometimes asleep.

A Nyul-Nyul informant told me how he doubted the claim of a medicine man to gain such information, so to test him, he asked him to ascertain when his (the questioner's) white employer was returning. He said that neither he nor the medicine man knew this. The latter went off a short distance and sat under a tree with the moonlight playing through the leaves and produced his "spirit-dogs," which the questioner actually saw. The medicine man sent these familiars on their errand and some little time later told him that as dawn came next morning he would hear the sound of his employer's horse approaching. Sure enough, this came to pass, confounding the unbelief of my informant.

Among the Wiradjeri (New South Wales), when the doctor lay down to rest, he would send his familiars (assistant totem) to other camps, irrespective of distance, to gain information of advantage to his own group. To do this, he would have to sing or "hum" or "think" his spirit out. He would often do this as he was dropping off to sleep. It has to be remembered that the distinction between the mind of the spirit-familiar and of the medicine man was only logical. The mind of one was the mind of the other. The spirit-familiar was an externalization of the man's spirit.

In such cases as the above, the medicine man seeks the distant information and does so through some psychic method while awake or while in a "pre-controlled" dream. But he is also capable of what we might call "picking up" information, as though thought waves and picture waves were coming through space and the trained medicine man was sensitive to them. The point to remember is that medicine men who specialize in such psychic practices claim that they are sensitive in this way, and tribesmen are satisfied with the results. Even when engaged in ordinary mundane affairs, doctors are on the alert to feel and notice psychic intimations, but from time to time they draw apart in mind and let the thoughts and impressions come.

One day a whole camp of Wiradjeri people was preparing and having their late afternoon meal, the result of the day's hunting. Two old medicine men were present, one lying down thinking, the other standing up. Suddenly the former jumped up and called out: "There is a mob coming to kill us, you had better all get together and get away!" and he pointed in the direction from which the attack would come. At about sundown all set out, the men fully armed—well, all except one old man who was skeptical, even when the clever man explained that he had seen it "in a vision." This old man changed his mind later and followed. The two doctors, by certain magical or mass hypnotic performances, caused the attackers to return to their own country.[13]

Many examples could be given of medicine men informing their people of the approach of friends or enemies and of what is happening at a distance.[14]

The Strong Eye

Medicine Man As Detective and Coroner

An important faculty that the clever men possess, and that is assiduously trained, is "the strong eye." This means not so much the power of looking into another person's mind as the power of looking into and through a sick person's body to see whether the soul is present or not, and also of being able to see the spirit of a "murderer" and even the spirits of the dead. In short, to possess the strong eye is to have the faculty of seeing spirits, of the living and of the dead.

In regions where soul stealing or soul wandering is a likely cause of illness, the diagnostician must have this power, and having seen that the patient's "vital" spirits (or principle) is missing, he must recover it. Prescribed actions and words convince the patient that the soul has been restored. He recovers.

Social sickness is fraught with consequences as serious as the illness of an individual. Indeed, it may be more disastrous, because it may be followed by disintegration of the whole group. This occurs when the serious illness, and especially the death of an individual, is believed to be caused by sorcery. In the former case, the effects of the sorcery must be neutralized. In the second, the "murderer" must be detected and revenge taken. In our own society, we may compare the sociopsychological effects of the appearance of a serious sickness of epidemic possibilities and the efforts to isolate and get rid of it.

In Aboriginal society, the medicine man, the man of high degree, is the detective and coroner. Many methods are used; for example, in the case of a death, the ground around the place of burial is inspected for marks showing the direction of the murderer's country; the exudations, bones, hair, or body of the dead person are examined or "asked" for a prescribed sign, the sign varying in different regions.[15]

In interpreting the signs and information, the coroner uses his general knowledge and careful observation. But the methods may be grouped into three classes. In the first, the departed person's spirit animates or guides the corpse, hair, bones, or exudations; the coroner need not see the spirit. In the other two classes, he must have the "strong eye," for either he sees the spirit of the dead person hanging around the murderer, or else he sees the latter's spirit hanging around the corpse, bones, or burial place of his victim. In exercising this strong sight, the medicine man may examine the corpse or burial place in some prescribed way, or he may gaze through the smoke of a ritual fire at a group that includes a likely sorcerer. Whatever the method, underlying it are the psychological facts that a murderer does sometimes feel the presence of his victim following him in an uncomfortable manner, and that a murderer sometimes feels constrained to revisit the scene of his crime.[16]

There is, however, another way in which a clever man uses the strong eye to discover the murderer—a way that is more psychical than the preceding. But only some medicine men practice it, for it involves clairvoyance. These men are usually known by a special term. One of them, a Murngin man, described his power by saying that he *knew* what had happened, whereas ordinary men could only *think* about it.

An interesting example comes from the Lower Murray region, where one of the worst forms of sorcery is fat-taking with the aid of a *thumi*. This is a long rope of human hair, into which the strength of the dying and dead persons has been made to pass, by having been wound around them. Operators, twelve in number, using this rope, wind it around their intended victim's body while he is asleep. They then hold the rope and all transmit the one suggestion to him, as a result of which he "comes" to them, so that they can extract his fat without leaving a mark. He revives, but later feels uneasy and ill, and suspects sorcery. His brother knows what has happened and sends for the specialist (*munkumbole*), for the usual healer fails. The specialist not only announces who took the fat, but also describes every detail of the preliminary reconnoitering and everything else. He says he can see all this in a vision.[17]

The decisions of the coroner can be difficult, because in many, if not in most, cases, it is probable that no one practiced any sorcery; there is no psychical reason, therefore, for any murderer's spirit to hang around the corpse, or for the spirit of the deceased to hang around the former, supposing such phenomena did occur. Moreover, it is probably stretching things too far to say that the death of a person, causing uneasiness in the mind of one who had wished the former's death but had suppressed the wish, results in the materialization of his personality attaching itself to the corpse or the materialization of the dead person attaching itself to him.

There is, however, the possibility that the coroner makes his decision in a logical manner on the basis of his wide knowledge of his fellows, and then either manipulates the accepted methods of divination or exercises psychic control over them and sees the spirit of the murderer or the murdered, as the case may be. The latter interpretation can be tentatively accepted, for it accords with the animistic and spiritistic view of life and death, and of human relations, that is accepted by all—including medicine men.

It is even possible to attribute honesty to the thumi fat-takers of the Lower Murray. The group of selected men led by a medicine man, a psychic expert, visualize the body of the victim; indeed, they give it a pseudomaterial form, which they draw to their laps, and on which they operate for the kidney fat, a cult-heroine closing the incision. Having passed through a ritual that directed their thoughts on their victim, and holding the rope of human hair, reinforced by spirits of the dead, they would be in a condition of acceptivity and ready to work out the leader's suggestion in trance. But that is not all; the Aborigines of southwest New South Wales and the Lower Murray maintain not only that they can remove the kidney fat of, or otherwise injure, a person's spirit-form, but also that this causes a corresponding effect on the material body of the victim.[18]

Psychic Displays

Many of the manifestations of psychic powers are for practical ends, to cure the sick, detect the sorcerer, gather information of social importance, visit the sky to release water stored there and so make rain, influence people at a distance, and protect the group. But in addition, specialists occasionally give displays of their power to impress on others the high degree of knowledge and power they have reached and so build up faith in their efficiency, an asset in the day of need. Initiations are favorite times for these exhibitions, no doubt because the young initiates are in a highly suggestible state and will be duly impressed. This definitely occurred in southeast Australia, where medicine men played a very important part in initiation.[19]

Walking on Fire

During one display in western New South Wales, after the bull-roarer had been swung, thus creating a mystic atmosphere, for it is the voice of Baiame (the sky cult-hero), the men present were told to sit around and stare into a big fire on the sacred ground. As they stared, they saw a clever man roll into the fire and scatter the coals. He then stood up among the rest of the men, who noticed that he was not burned, nor were the European clothes that he wore damaged. The informant and the others were quite satisfied the doctor was in the fire. In 1944 some Weilwan men told me that they had seen this same doctor "walk through the fire" naked and unhurt.

Aborigines, on ceremonial occasions, are able, in their excitement, to stamp on and scatter the burning coals of a fire without any apparent harm, and novices in initiation are sometimes tossed into a big smoke fire. But these displays of fire-rolling and fire-walking were thought to go further. It is, moreover, in line with the claim and the belief that medicine men can travel in a flame of fire or send fire from their bodies along invisible cords to objects to which they had attached the cords. This power arose from a flame of fire having been sung into them by Baiame at their making.[20]

The Use of Magic Cord

During their making in southeast Australia, a magic cord is slung into the doctors. This cord becomes a means of performing marvelous feats, such as sending fire from the medicine man's insides, like an electric wire. But even more interesting is the use made of the cord to travel up to the sky or to the tops of trees through space. At the display during initiation—a time of ceremonial excitement—the doctor lies on his back under a tree, sends his cord up, and climbs up it to a nest on top of the tree, then across to other trees, and at sunset, down to the ground again. Only men saw this performance, and it is preceded and followed by the swinging of the bull-roarers and other expressions of emotional excitement.[21] In the descriptions of these performances recorded by R. M. Berndt and myself, the names of the doctors are given and such details as the following: Joe Dagan, a Wongaibon clever man, lying on his back at the foot of a tree, sent his cord directly up, and "climbed" up with his head well back, body outstretched, legs apart, and arms to his sides. Arriving at the top, twelve meters up, he waved his arms to those below, then came down in the same manner, and while still on his back the cord re-entered his body.

Apparently, in this case, his body floated up and down in the horizontal position with no movement of his hands or legs, and the explanation must be sought in group suggestion of a powerful nature.[22]

Disappearing and Reappearing

Another form of psychic display was to disappear from one spot suddenly and appear in another, or to pass into or out of a tree. Thus one man (J. K.) said that at his initiation, a clever doctor (C. J.) was standing near the novices, when quite suddenly he disappeared, and then was seen standing with his back to them about 140 meters away, turning from time to time to look at them. "He was doing this to show them all he was very clever."

Another doctor hit a tree and disappeared into it, like stone sinking into muddy water. The reverse of this is given in the following episode: J. K. was about to doze off one morning while the billy was boiling, when he was awakened by an iguana touching his foot. Looking at it, he noticed that it turned its head around in the direction of some trees. So he sang out to his two brothers who were nearby, "That old fellow (M. D.) must be about here," for he knew that M. D. had an iguana inside him (that is, as a familiar). Standing up, he looked at the iguana, which suddenly ran back to a tree and disappeared. From this, they knew that M. D. must be inside that tree. Then they heard M. D. call out in a low voice, "Can you see me?" But they could not, until he gradually came out of the tree, which closed up without leaving a mark. He then walked up to them and said he had sent out his spirit helper to see whether they would recognize it.

Aborigines regarded dreams as material occurrences, and this may have been a dream experience. The narrator, however, says he was wide awake; if so, the clever fellow (M. D.) must have exercised some psychical power over the three men.

Creating Illusions

Another incident illustrates the power of creating illusions in the minds of a group, but this time not merely for display but to protect one's own group. Two medicine men, having sent their group on ahead, lit a big fire and, lying like logs on either side, sang a magical song. The enemy saw and heard them, but when they rushed in and speared the "men," the singing stopped, and they saw only two logs. In the distance they could see the two doctors walking along. After this experience had been repeated several times, the enemy realized that they were being played with by very clever men and so went home.

This may be only an elaboration of an able elusion of an enemy raiding party, and wonders apart, medicine men usually did play an important part on both the raiding and the defending sides. Magical help was essential.[23]

Fast Traveling

Medicine men are believed to be able to travel at a very fast pace. This is obvious enough if the claim is to fly in sleep or in a vision to distant places, or to send their familiars on such journeys. But they can also run at a surprising pace for any distance, faster than anyone can run, and without getting tired or out of breath. They apparently run less than a meter above the ground. Indeed, it has been said that the air has been made soft and solid, and that it moves along, carrying them with it. The explanation given by other Aborigines is that "these clever men can make their spirits take them along very quickly." Information regarding this form of progression comes from southeast Australia, especially western New South Wales, and eastern South Australia.[24]

Aborigines are noted for their extraordinary feats of walking long distances, at what we regard as remarkable speed. Hunting and raiding on foot fits them for this. But the medicine man's powers are said to exceed this and to be more than physical.

Meditation

At the back of these claims to various psychic powers, for whatever they are worth, is the fact that Aborigines spend much time with their own thoughts, reflecting on dreams, and being ready, at any moment, to enter a condition of receptivity. The quietness and silence of so much of their life, the absence of rush and of urgent appointments, and the fewness of their numbers facilitate this occupation with the psychic. Moreover, their totemistic and animistic view of life predisposes them to it.

Some persons, however, specialize in meditation as well as in psychic experiences. All men of high degree have practiced it, but some do so to the exclusion of becoming adepts in other branches of magical and psychical endeavor. The temptation is to think that an Aborigine sitting down, apparently dreaming, is doing nothing. But he may be engaged in serious meditational and psychic discipline. It is to this aspect of their life that I desire to draw special attention.

The following is a description by an Aboriginal informant of an old man meditating. It is translated freely from the native text in Yaralde.[25]

> When you see an old man sitting by himself over here in the camp, do not disturb him, for if you do he will "growl" at you. Do not play near him, because he is sitting down by himself with his thoughts in order "to see." He is gathering those thoughts so that he can feel and hear. Perhaps he then lies down, getting into a special posture, so that he may see when sleeping. He sees indistinct visions and hears "persons" talk in them. He gets up and looks for those he has seen, but, not seeing them, he lies down again in the prescribed manner, so as to see what he had seen before. He puts his head on the pillow as previously so as to see [have a vision] as before. Getting up, he tells his friends to strengthen that power [miwi] within them, so that when they lie down they will see and feel [or become aware of] people not present, and in that way they will perceive them.

This describes how certain persons, abstracting themselves from what was happening around them and concentrating on the psychic power within them, practiced something akin to recollection. Lying down in the prescribed posture, they saw and "heard" what was happening at a distance. In other words, they were clairvoyant. Indeed, during such periods of meditation and vision, when this power and his own thoughts were as one, the clever man would see visions unconnected with earthly life. He would go to the world of ancestral beings.

This power, called *miwi* by the Yaralde of the Lower Murray, is said to be present in all persons but to be especially developed by a few. All manifestations of psychic power are dependent on it—including white and black magic. Old people can use it so as to know who is coming and what is going to happen, whereas the especially gifted person, after much practice, can perform the quite remarkable acts already described. This miwi is said to be located in the pit of the stomach. And even as I wrote this, at Walgett, in August 1944, among the Weilwan tribal remnants there, I was told how they seem to know events of importance to them before it seems feasible that they should do so. And several of them have told me that the clever man (*wiringin*) sent something out of his body (pointing to the stomach) to see things. Moreover, this something might even be a materialization of himself, which could be seen by at least some persons kilometers away where it had been "sent," such persons being sensitives.

Comparison with Tibet

Some light on our Aboriginal men of high degree can be obtained by a comparison with those from Tibet, a country characterized by psychic specialization. There the great yogi, possessed of clairvoyant vision, is said to be able to observe the physiological processes of his own body. He requires no mechanical devices in order to traverse air or water or land, for he tells us that he can quit his gross physical body and visit any part of the earth or pass beyond the stratosphere to other worlds with a speed greater than light. As a result of his discipline and training, he can acquire fleetness of foot, lightness of body, and immunity to harm by fire. He can become immune also to severe cold, the result of practicing the yoga of psychic heat. This includes concentration and visualization of fire at the meeting point of the nerves at the psychic center. The latter is situated four fingers below the navel. It is "the hidden abode of the sleeping Goddess Kundalini, the personification of the Serpent-Power, of the latent mystic fire-force of the body."[26] And there, too, are located the miwi, the cord, and the rainbow serpent or other familiar in the case of the Australian man of high degree.

Let us remember, too, one of the favorite exercises of the yogi, the "man of the rule": sitting in a prescribed way on a prescribed type of couch, gazing at the end of his nose and not looking around about him, he becomes impassive to the perceptions of the senses and enjoys boundless happiness.[27]

Psychic Terrors

To reach that high degree of psychic power by which one can send power out to bring death or life, to gain knowledge and to transfer thought without any hindrance of time or space, and to see visions requires much practice, courage, and perseverance. Dangers and terrors must be faced—dangers of a psychic nature, the creation probably of one's own psychic exercise or perception. The following describes the experience to be expected by a Yaralde postulant (Lower Murray):[28]

> When you lie down to see the prescribed visions, and you do see them, do not be frightened, because they will be horrible. They are hard to describe, though they are in my mind and my *miwi*, and though I could project the experience into you after you had been well trained.
>
> However, some of them are evil spirits, some are like snakes, some are like horses with men's heads, and some are spirits of evil men which resemble burning fires. You see your camp burning and the flood waters rising, and thunder, lightning, and rain, the earth rocking, the hills moving, the waters whirling, and the trees which still

> stand, swaying about. Do not be frightened. If you get up, you will not see these scenes, but when you lie down again, you will see them, unless you get too frightened. If you do, you will break the web [or thread] on which the scenes are hung. You may see dead persons walking toward you, and you will hear their bones rattle. If you hear and see these things without fear, you will never be frightened of anything. These dead people will not show themselves to you again because your *miwi* [psychic force] is now strong. You are now powerful because you have seen these dead people.

In this we have a psychic explanation of postulants sleeping on graves, in some cases eating a small portion of a dead person's body, and so going to the sky and the spirits of the dead, of being met and killed by spirits and powerful beings of various types, and of having one's insides taken out, and even of being eaten or swallowed. I have met several persons who failed. At the sight of the ghost, they struggled and fled.

In Tibet, those who aspire to be great magicians and lamas, after long and hard training in ritual, words, and dance, may become the subject of a mystic banquet. The postulant goes alone to a burial place or any wild site whose physical aspect awakens feelings of terror, especially one associated with a terrible legend or a recent tragic event. A place of this type is chosen for the rite so that the occult forces of conscious beings believed to be associated with such places will come into operation during the performance. After the mystic preliminaries the lonely celebrant, who is in an intense state of excitement, calls the demons to feast on himself. He imagines that a feminine deity, who esoterically personifies his own will, cuts off his head, severs his limbs, skins him, and rips open his abdomen. His insides fall out, and his blood flows like a river, providing a feast for his hideous guests. Hypnotized by the ritual, he urges them on with liturgical words of unreserved surrender. At length, this "red meal" comes to an end, the vision vanishes, utter loneliness follows, and the exaltation aroused by the dramatic sacrifice gradually subsides. And the candidate has passed to another stage of enlightenment and psychic power.[29] This reminds us of the abdominal operation in the ritual making of Aboriginal men of high degree.

Ritual Cannibalism

Some of the Tibetan occultists are also believed to practice ritual cannibalism, but in esoteric teaching this is associated with a doctrine of transubstantiation. Some human beings "have attained such high degree of spiritual perfection that the original material substance of their bodies has been transmuted into a more subtle one which possesses special qualities. A morsel of their transformed flesh, when eaten, will produce a special kind of ecstasy and bestow knowledge and supernatural powers upon the person partaking of it."[30] So it is with the Aboriginal postulant in some regions. He partakes of the corpse and in a mystic way sees the dead or visits the sky, thus deriving power and knowledge.[31]

Rapid Traveling

In Tibet, too, certain lamas, as a result of physical and psychical training, are able to tramp at a rapid pace and without stopping for quite long periods. One of these, as seen by Mrs. David-Neel, proceeded at an unusual gait and with extraordinary swiftness. Her servants begged her not to stop him, because the lamas, when traveling, must not stop their meditation. If they did so, the "god" in them would escape, and they would die. The fact is that a *lung-gom-pa* traveler ran in a kind of trance, and a sudden awakening would painfully disturb his nerves. Actually, the man did not run, but seemed to lift himself from the ground, proceeding by leaps or bounds, with the regularity of a pendulum. Another of these "runners" seen by this author proceeded up a hill toward her party at an extraordinary pace, but when he arrived he was not out of breath. He seemed to be only half conscious. The trance, however, gradually subsided. Mrs. David-Neel is convinced that as a result of the physical training and the training in self-hypnosis a condition is reached in which "one does not feel the weight of one's body. A kind of anaesthesia deadens the sensations that would be produced by knocking against the stones or other obstacles on the way, and one walks for hours at an unaccustomed speed, enjoying that kind of light agreeable dizziness well known to motorists at high speed." Some of the initiates claim that eventually, "after he has travelled over a certain distance, the feet of the 'runner' no longer touch the ground, and that he glides on the air with an extreme celerity"[32]—a striking parallel to the power attributed to Australian medicine men.

Telepathy

The telepathy that the Aboriginal men of high degree practice is also practiced by the Tibetan psychic adepts. The Tibetans "assert that telepathy is a science, which can be learnt like any other science, by those who have proper teaching and are fit instruments to put the theory into practice.[33] The adepts ascribe the cause of the phenomena to intense concentration of thought, requiring a mastery over the mind so as to produce "one-pointedness of thought." Moreover, the conscious receiver must have "tuned in" to receive or "pick up" the thought waves. This demands the faculty of emptying one's mind of all ideas, reflections, and mental images and of discriminating among the various images, moods, feelings, and influences that arise or appear. Some experts claim to be able to read the thoughts of others as well, and some to convey messages to complete strangers. Needless to say, years are devoted to these practices, and, undoubtedly, according to some reliable observers, success is gained.

Mrs. David-Neel suggests that the extraordinary silence and solitude of Tibet offers favorable conditions for telepathy.[34] I have long thought that the silence and solitude of the Australian bush, the absence of the noise and bustle of crowds, the lack of hurry, and the long hours with little to do were conditions favorable to meditation and receptivity, to tuning in with the world and to conjuring up pictures of persons and events not present. Sometimes the old white bushman or the Aborigine "just sits," but sometimes he "just sits and thinks," and to the latter at least the thinking may include receiving; for the man of high degree, it may include "sending messages on the wind," to use a Tibetan phrase.

Sometimes the message as received is a vision, a materialization, and whether in Tibet or in Aboriginal Australia, that vision is no mere hallucination. It is a mental formation visualized and externalized, which may even exist for a time independent of its creator. Visions, too, which are sought, must be distinguished from dreams. While the person is experiencing the vision, he cannot move, but he is conscious of what is going on around him. As one man of high degree of the Kattang tribe, New South Wales, told me concerning his making: he could see and know what was happening, but was as one dead, feeling nothing.

A fully initiated man of the Weilwan tribe informed me that while camped with his wife on a sheep station where he was working, he had seen his father-in-law, a clever man, standing just outside their tent. His wife, however, could not see the latter, although he said to her, "That old fellow is out there." Actually, the clever man was away at his own camp but admitted later that he was at that time also outside my informant's tent. He always knew when the latter was returning from his various places of employment. Apparently, those two were en rapport with each other, so that my informant "saw" the materialization of the clever man, and his mind was open to the latter, even at a distance.

An incident similar to this was described by another informant. W—, a doctor, was with some other Aborigines at the horseyard on a station where they were working. When the rest set out for the camp, about 400 meters away, he remained at the yard, saying that he would catch up to them. When they reached their camp, however, he was sitting there making a boomerang, as though he had not been away. They did not see him pass, and there was no hidden track by which he could have hurried around. The question arises, was he at the horseyard in the flesh, or did he cause the others to see a materialization of himself there? My informant was one of those involved in the incident.

Such phenomena are reported from Tibet. Both Mrs. David-Neel and one of her servants saw independently and together a young Tibetan employee walking by himself toward the camp early in the morning and wearing an unusual hat. He went behind a rock, and as he did not reappear, the place was searched, but no sign of him was found. Just before dusk that day he arrived with his caravan and wearing the strange hat. Careful inquiries revealed that he had not been away from it. Mrs. David-Neel suggests that this was a kind of thought-form creation or visualization but apparently generated unconsciously by the young man.

This same author refers to a striking incident at the consecration of the Tashilumpo monastery by the aged Kyongbu. He got into the sedan-chair that was sent for him, and which was closed and escorted. But to the astonishment of the thousands waiting at the monastery, he was seen coming alone and on foot. He walked straight up to a giant Buddha-image and gradually became incorporated in it. When the sedan-chair arrived at the monastery, it was found to be empty. Circumstances prevented Mrs. David-Neel from examining on the spot whether collective hallucination or some other phenomenon was involved, but the capacity on the part of certain persons of being "seen" in more than one place at one time is not doubted.[35]

Secret Cults and Religion

I have referred to Tibetan occult practices principally because those of Aboriginal Australia seem to be of the same order, even if not so highly developed. They may even have degenerated from a common source. In any case, the practices are less systematized in Australia, at least partly because of the absence of written records. During recent years, a serious endeavor has been made to study Tibetan phenomena in a scientific manner, and as a result we may derive from them some understanding of the Australian phenomena.

It is possible that there is some historical connection between the yoga and occult practices of India and Tibet and the practices and psychic powers of Aboriginal men of high degree. Hinduism spread to the East Indies. Yoga is a cult in Bali, and some of the remarkable feats of the Australian medicine men are paralleled by their fellow professionals in Papua.[36]

Moreover, the Aborigines hold the doctrines of preexistence and of reincarnation, which suggest a northern source, just as the distribution of their practice of circumcision and of tree-stage burial ritual suggests an influence from the East Indies.

Apart from the interesting problem of origin, Australian Aboriginal religion, with its emphasis on mysteries and degrees of initiation, its doctrines of pre-existence and reincarnation, and its belief in psychic powers, belongs to the Orient, not to the West, and can only be understood in the light of the Orient. In the past, the custom has been to study and judge Aboriginal religion and magic from the point of view of the Occident. We have found the external universe of overwhelming interest and sought, with much success, its explanation in mechanical and physical laws. Elated by our success, we have endeavored with limited enthusiasm to apply those same laws to man as an individual and as a social being, and to the problems of life, consciousness, and death. This was praiseworthy, but it is possible that this approach has led to our neglecting or to considering as unworthy or unscientific certain phenomena that men have claimed to be important and potent. Many of us have tended to regard members of the Society for Psychical Research as queer beings. But it is scientific to study all phenomena, and to do so patiently, objectively, and, if necessary, with new approaches. And the powers of the human mind are worthy of such investigation. At least, we need to understand the self, that is, ourselves.

We of the West are so intellectual, so rational, in our approach to religion that we have inhibited real freedom of thought with regard to religion. The Orient, however, so Dr. Evans-Wentz claims, is scientifically experimental in religion. It studies the ramifications and possibilities of the mind in the psychic sphere and boldly experiments and makes inductions. The same writer maintains that "anthropology and psychology as applied sciences in the sense understood in Yoga are for almost all Occidental scientists mere dreams of impracticable visionaries." And he adds, as a result of twenty-five years of research, that he does not believe that this unsound view can long endure.[37] Our approach is the academic and rational one of Greek philosophers and the West. The Oriental approach is one of experiment and observation.

Conclusion

The purpose of these two chapters, however, has not been to make claims on behalf of psychic practices or research—I have no knowledge in such a field. I have only recorded and analyzed phenomena, claims, and beliefs. My object has been to show, first, that Aboriginal medicine men, so far from being rogues, charlatans, or ignoramuses, are men of high degree, that is, men who have taken a degree in the secret life beyond that taken by most adult males—a step that implies discipline, mental training, courage, and perseverance; second, that they are men of respected, and often of outstanding, personality; third, that they are of immense social significance, the psychological health of the group largely depending on faith in their powers; fourth, that the various psychic powers attributed to them must not be too readily dismissed as mere primitive magic and "make-believe," for many of them have specialized in the working of the human mind and in the influence of mind on body and of mind on mind; fifth, that the ritual of "death and rising" by which they receive their powers includes and causes a deep psychological experience; and last, that as long as they observe the customary discipline of their "order," this experience continues to be a source of faith to themselves and their fellows.

In brief, Aboriginal men of high degree are a channel of life.

Notes

1. C. Baudouin, *Suggestion and Auto-Suggestion* (Hackensack, N.J.: Wehmar Bros., 1922), p. 244.
2. W. Ramsay Smith, *Myths and Legends of the Australian Aboriginals* (London: G. G. Harrap, 1930), pp. 186–89. This general description is for the Yaralde and other groups of the Lower Murray River, South Australia. Smith records it under the heading *Neilyeri*. Taplin (in J. D. Woods, 29–31) described this as a deadly poisonous implement, with which a victim is pricked.

3. Spencer and Gillen, *Native Tribes*, pp. 531–32.
4. G. N. M. Tyrrell, *Science and Psychical Phenomena* (London: Methuen, 1938), p. 63.
5. Ramsay Smith, *Myths and Legends*, pp. 202–5. Taplin, in Woods, pp. 23–26, gives only a superficial account of this form of pointing. I have referred to the qualifications required by a person desirous of using special pointing bones in *Australian Aborigines*, pp. 312–13.
6. S. Freud, *Totem and Taboo*, translated by R. R. Brill (London: Routledge, 1919), chapter 3.
7. Tyrell, *Science and Psychical Phenomena*, pp. 54–55.
8. R. M. Berndt, in personal correspondence.
9. Power, or *miwi*, will be discussed later.
10. Warner, *Black Civilization*, p. 214.
11. See, for example, the Wiradjeri, Kakadu, Mandjinda, and Aluridja in chapters 3 and 4.
12. Tyrrell, *Science and Psychical Phenomena*, p. 54.
13. From a special report by R. M. Berndt. The doctor who had the vision was the grandfather of Berndt's informant.
14. For examples of clairvoyance and suchlike, see Warner, *Black Civilization*, p. 251. Webb, "Making of a Marrngit," p. 339. Elkin, "Notes on Psychic Life," pp. 49–56; also unpublished field notes; Weilwan and Kamilaroi clever men, 1944.
15. Elkin, *Australian Aborigines*, pp. 343–49.
16. H. M. Moran, *Viewless Winds* (London: P. Davies, 1939), p. 241. Howitt, *Native Tribes*, p. 371, refers to the belief that the "fat-taker" watches at the scene of the murder.
17. Ramsay Smith, *Myths and Legends*, pp. 191, 198–200. Strangely enough, the specialist says that the stricken man's elder brother can see this vision but cannot tell anyone about it.
18. This is inherent in the totemic conception of (a) the totem being the flesh of the totemite, and (b) of the, or a, totem representing the totemite in dreams and visions. The appearance of the totem in special or untoward circumstances is associated with the presence of the spirit-form of the person represented by the totem. To injure the totem is to injure the totemite, and this can be done in dream and vision even more efficiently than in daily life. B. Spencer and F. J. Gillen, *The Arunta* (London: Macmillan, 1927), vol. 1., p. 80: "The totem of any man is regarded . . . as the same thing as himself." Elkin, *Australian Aborigines*, pp. 185, 187. Howitt, *Native Tribes*, pp. 145–48. R. M. Berndt, unpublished report. K. L. Parker, *The Euahlayi Tribe* (London: Constable, 1905), p. 29. Howitt, *Native Tribes*, p. 373, quotes a Wurunjerri: "Sometimes men only know about having their fat taken by remembering something of it as in a dream."

19. In central and northwestern regions, headmen of local totemic cult-clans, or lodges, take the lead in arranging series of totemic ceremonies for the education of the newly initiated. These ceremonies are concerned with the eternal dreamtime and its heroes. The doctors do not, as such, play a leading part in these ceremonies. However, in the southeast, by virtue of their special association with the sky cult-hero and with the spirits of the dead, they did seem to act as the real masters of the ceremonies. See Howitt, *Native Tribes*, chapter 9 passim, and compare Spencer and Gillen, *Northern Tribes*, chapters 7 to 9, which describe initiation ceremonies but make no mention of medicine men. Howitt refers to the constant display by the medicine men of their magic powers during initiation ceremonies. "On Some Australian Ceremonies of Initiation," *Journal of the Royal Anthropological Institute*, London 13:445–46, 450.
20. Compare the ceremonial Fijian and Malay fire walking, which does occur in actual fact.
21. Including a ritual exchange of women.
22. This information was gathered by R. M. Berndt for the Wiradjeri and other tribes, "Wuradjeri Magic and Clever Men," *Oceania* 17, no. 4:340–44. Howitt referred to this use of cords and the power of traveling through the air. And I recorded the belief that the Forrest River medicine man climbed to the sky on a cord. See chapters 3 and 4.
23. Howitt, *Native Tribes*, p. 374, refers to the belief in the power of medicine men to turn themselves into stumps, etc., and so avoid capture.
24. R. M. Berndt, "Wuradjeri Magic," p. 357. Ramsay Smith, *Myths and Legends*, p. 191. The operators in thumi sorcery walk on air, which the spirits have made soft and solid for a foot above the earth. The air also moves, carrying the operators direct to their victim. Billy Emu, a famous Weilwan clever fellow, was able to cover 112 kilometers a day, as fast as horsemen. Elkin, Field Notes, 1944.
25. The Yaralde is a Lower Murray River tribe. Text recorded by R. M. Berndt.
26. W. Y. Evans-Wentz, *Tibetan Yoga and Secret Doctrines* (Oxford: Oxford University Press, 1935 and 1958), pp. 23–24, 199. In Bali, where yoga is practiced, the secret invisible fire (*geni rahasya*) is said to be located in the navel. W. Weck, *Heikunde und Volkstum auf Bali*, (1937), p. 232.
27. *Bhagavad Gita*, translated by L. D. Barnett (London: Temple Classics, 1941), pp. 113–15, 188–89.
28. R. M. Berndt, in personal correspondence.
29. Alexandra David-Neel, *With Mystics and Magicians in Tibet* (Harmondsworth: Penguin), pp. 139–54. For the yoga text, Evans-Wentz, *Tibetan Yoga*, pp. 301–18.
30. Ibid., p. 126.
31. For example: The Wiimbaio, Ta-ta-thi, Barkinji, and Wampangee. See chapter 3.
32. David-Neel, *With Mystics and Magicians*, pp. 183–97.

33. Ibid., p. 211. Evans-Wentz, *Tibetan Yoga*, p. 178, says that the art of transferring thought and visualizations has long been known to the masters of the occult sciences of the Orient.
34. David-Neel, *With Mystics and Magicians*, pp. 210–15 and 215–20, for Mrs. David-Neel's personal experiences.
35. David-Neel, *With Mystics and Magicians*, pp. 139, 180, 279–80, 285–88. Just before his death, the famous Tibetan yogi Milarepa was seen in different places by different people at the same time, in each case performing appropriate acts. W. Y. Evans-Wentz, *Tibet's Great Yogi, Milarepa* (Oxford: Oxford University Press, 1969), 2nd edition, pp. 286–89. This author says that "the Perfected Yogi possesses the power of reproducing his phenomenal physical body in countless numbers, one such body in one place or world, another in another." Ibid., p. 269, fn. 1.
36. Williams, *Papuans of the Trans-Fly*, p. 342. Weck, *Heikunde und Volkstum auf Bali*, pp. 231–37, describes the application of yoga practices to healing in Bali.
37. Evans-Wentz, *Tibetan Yoga*, pp. 48–50.

PART II

The Making and Powers —A Survey

CHAPTER 3

The Uncircumcision Regions

Plan of Survey

This (1944) survey of our knowledge of the making of medicine men and of their powers commences with eastern Australia, working from south to north and keeping within the region of the uncircumcised tribes; this includes the area south of and adjacent to the Murray River, all New South Wales except the far northwestern corner, and Queensland with the exception of its far west. The information is then given for the uncircumcision area of Western Australia, which lies west of a line joining Wollal to Esperance. The circumcision region is then surveyed, proceeding from South Australia and the neighboring region of Western Australia to the Northern Territory and far western Queensland, and finally the Kimberley Division of Western Australia.

This geographical approach is partly one of convenience, but it also recognizes the fact that medicine men, being men of high degree, are not made until they have passed through the degrees that all men must take. In the circumcision region, these include the ordeal and mark of circumcision and, in most parts, of subincision also, but the other regions have not been affected by the diffusion of this comparatively recent rite and its mythology. It has yet to be shown whether the presence or absence of circumcision in initiation has any close relation to the type of ritual for making medicine men, or to their powers. There is, however, one interesting correlation. In the uncircumcised regions, the operations and most impressive experiences are said usually to occur during a trance, seldom when dead, whereas in the circumcision region, the central experience is frequently described as one of death or of being killed. In these regions, circumcision is a ritual act of killing.

The survey proceeds from south to north because an analysis of mythology and ritual suggests that diffusion has been on the whole in the opposite direction. Therefore, by proceeding northward, we may meet traits that either were dropped on the way or that, being somewhat recent, had not yet spread all the way south.

South of the Murray

The Aborigines on the Lower Murray and around Encounter Bay had their clever men, but, although our earliest informants, the missionaries Taplin and Meyer, recorded interesting details about forms of sorcery practiced in the region, they gathered no information of value regarding the doctors. Taplin wrote in 1873, "There used to be a class of doctors amongst the natives called *kuldukke* men. They were great impostors." Meyer wrote that every tribe had its own doctor, who had only one remedy for every disease; but each doctor had a different one, namely the object, animal, or vegetable that he regarded as his friend or protector. Thus, one had a snake, another an ant, another seaweed, and so on. This "friend" (apparently, an assistant-totem or familiar) seems to have helped the doctor during the process of sucking the afflicted part of the patient's body.[1]

During fieldwork for the Australian National Research Council, R. M. Berndt recorded native texts that show that among these people there was a class of clever men who specialized in meditation, hypnotism, thought transference, and "seeing" what was occurring at a distance. They could even, by their psychic powers, turn sorcerers from contemplated evil acts. They could travel through the air on a cord (projected from their own bodies), take the form of any natural species, and make themselves invisible. Their making occupied several years, but the details are not known. These were probably similar to those recorded for the Wiradjeri and neighboring tribes in the Riverina.

In the Gunditj-Mara and related tribes of southwestern Victoria, the doctor can summon the aid of a spirit in his curative work by going up to the clouds and bringing the spirit down. Apparently a seance is held. The men sit in a circle around a tree and the patient. Then the doctor and the spirit alight on top of the tree and from there jump to the ground with a thud. "The spirit gives his name; and after the doctor has felt all over the body of his patient, they both go up to the clouds again." The patient recovers. In illness the sick person's spirit may go away, but the doctor can bring it down with him in the form of a doll, which produces a moaning noise. The doctor presses the doll to the patient's chest to let the spirit return to the body. Sometimes in cases of severe illness, the doctor brings down ten spirits, who advise him regarding the treatment.

Occasionally, a doctor gives a display of his occult powers at the conclusion of a corroboree. He summons three or four female spirits, who dance around the fire and announce their names as those of deceased members of the tribe. Anybody can look at these spirits, but only the doctor can speak to them.[2]

The medicine men of the Wotjobaluk and Jupagalk tribes of northwestern Victoria are made by a supernatural being named Ngatya, who lives in the bush. He opens the postulant's side and inserts in it such objects as quartz crystals, which give medicine men their power. This includes fat-taking. They cut open the victim's right side, extract fat, then bring the edges of the wound together and, singing a spell, make them join without leaving a scar. Further singing causes the man to rise up, and at the same time a star falls from the sky with the man's heart. The same practice and belief exist among the Mukjarawaint and Jajauring. There is therefore an association between the medicine man's surgical act and the sky. Indeed, although he is said to be made by a spirit living in the bush, he is henceforth connected with the sky-world. The Wotjobaluk say that Bunjil, a great man who was once on earth and who is spoken of as "Our Father," lives in some place beyond the sky. It is beyond the Wurk-Kerun or dark place, which the medicine men say is like a mountain. They can only go as far as this mountain, where they are met by Gargomitch, who takes their enquiries on to Bunjil. They probably reached the sky by way of a pine tree that extended through the sky to the latter's abode.[3]

The medicine men of these tribes were associated in another way with the sky. Some of them were seers, and among the Mukjarawaint, these had great influence "because of their power of communicating with the departed, up to whom they went." The home of the dead, according to the Kulin, was in the sky, which was reached by the rays of the setting sun. Indeed, in this tribe the power to see ghosts was a necessary qualification for training, which was given by a medicine man. Part of the process consisted of smoking the novice with the leaves of the native cherry tree and of anointing him with red ochre and grease. These were public acts; the real training was not ascertained.[4]

Jajauring medicine men were made in the world of spirits, which the individual visited for two or three days while in a trance.[5] Those of the Wurunjeri tribe received their magical powers from the sky-being Bunjil, to whom they were carried by ghosts through a hole in the sky. Their powers included the extraction of "fat,"[6] the use of many magical substances, especially quartz, and the power of going invisibly through space up to the sky and beyond it to Tharangalkbek, the "gum tree" country. In order to counteract a certain type of contagious magic, the medicine man had to secure the spear-thrower that had been used in that process and take it to this land beyond the sky, where it was put in water. The ascent was made by a cord through a hole in the vault. This sky-country is also the home of the dead and is the place to which Bunjil ascended with all his people, after having taught the Kulin the arts of life. He instituted the dual organization at the request of two medicine men. The Wurunjeri medicine men are therefore associated with the spirits of the dead, the sky-world, and Bunjil, the tribal All-Father.[7]

The Kurnai, who occupied almost the whole of Gippsland, distinguish between the medicine men and the Birraark. The latter were likened to seers, spirit-mediums, and bards. They were initiated by ghosts in the bush and had to wear a nose bone by which the ghosts could convey them through the clouds. They were admitted at the entrance to the sky by the headman of the Sky-Land, where they saw people dancing and learned new songs and dances, which they afterward taught to the Kurnai. Ghosts also came and spoke to them, as in a seance.[8]

Medicine men proper were made by the ancestral ghosts in dreams. This was done in two ways; in one, the ghosts came and communicated both harmful and protective chants and knowledge. They were shown quartz crystals and a magical object, *bulk.*[9] The other method was similar, with the addition that the novice's education was completed elsewhere. For example, one individual, after dreaming of his father three times, was carried by a cord tied around his neck and waist, to Wilson's Promontory.[10] There he was blindfolded and led into a great cave, where it was as bright as day. All the old men were round about. The initiate's father showed him a lot of shining things on the wall and told him to take some. He was taught outside the cave how to make them go in and out of his legs. The ghosts then carried him back and left him up in a tree, where he found himself on waking. He was able to throw the shining things received in the cave, "like light in the evening."[11]

Objective reality was attributed to dreams by the Kurnai,[12] but even so, the description of the making of their medicine men cannot be dismissed as only a dream experience. Even were that possible, the elements of the dream would have to be accounted for. It is reasonable to suggest that the visit to the cave, the seeing of the old men and the shining objects, the receiving of instruction in using the latter, and the ritual burial in a tree had objective reality. The making must have included a period of seclusion in which the candidate received his power and instruction, and during part of which he was no doubt in a state of exhaustion and trance. The details of the trance experience would be prepared for and controlled. Finally, the power of using magical substances, and of taking human fat, was no mere dream.[13]

The mountains of Wilson's Promontory, moreover, were the home of Lohan, who, according to a legend preserved by the Wurunjeri, came with his people from the Yarra by way of Western Port to Corner Inlet. From the mountains, he watches over his people, and the Kurnai believe that he makes their country deadly to strangers. He can still be seen. The person wishing to see him must first obtain the consent of the Yarra people, sit for a whole day fasting and facing a fire, and then perform special ablutions for two or three days. The visitor is painted when about a day's journey from Lohan's special bit of country, which lies between Hoddle's Creek and the Promontory. Finally, in the early morning he is conducted with downcast eyes, by some of Lohan's own men who have been with him all through, to a spot from which Lohan is seen for a moment—"clothed in mist and regarding with unnatural but human eyes these intruders—and all is over." "He indicates through his young men that he is pleased with the strangers. They have been obedient to his laws. Ever after, by the power of Loo-ern (Lohan), the strangers can kill all enemies, except those belonging to Loo-ern's country."[14] This seems to refer to an initiation ceremony, by which individuals are made members of a group associated with a former tribal leader. It does not appear to refer especially to medicine men, but it does show that the Kurnai dream-method of making medicine men in a cave on the Promontory can reasonably be regarded as something more than fantasy or only a dream experience.

The Coast of New South Wales

The source of magical power in the Ngarigo, Wolgal, and Yuin tribes in the southeast of New South Wales is Daramulan, the culture-hero and sky-being. Training is given by the medicine men. The powers include the use of magical substances, especially quartz crystals, which are indeed given by Daramulan. Thus, quartz is definitely associated with the sky-being. The extraction of human fat is also practiced by the medicine men. The wound made in this operation is closed up without leaving a mark.[15]

The medicine men of the Port Jackson tribe obtained their powers by sleeping at the grave of a deceased person. The spirit of the latter seized the aspirant by the throat, opened him, and took out his bowels, which he replaced, after which the wound closed up.[16] The Geawe-gal, who occupied part of Hunter Valley, are reported to have had medicine men who were in communication with supernatural influence. The Port Stephens medicine men were generally the only persons to see Koin, the sky All-Father. The Gringai around Dungog believed that fat extraction was practiced by medicine men of hostile tribes.[17]

For the Kattang-speaking people who occupied the northern shore of Port Stephens and the country up to Taree, I learned from a karadji (clever man) that a postulant must have gone through the high initiation degree of *Bumban*, which took about six months and included a severe fire ceremony and the revelation of a number of important symbols. The candidate "died" at this ceremony, being thrown on the fire by men, then lifted up and kept over the fire until it was burned out. Actually, the candidate felt nothing because he was in a condition approaching hypnosis, though he could see what was there. He was restored by the old men putting their hands on his shoulder, after which he was shown secret symbols and taught their meaning. As a result, the man became a new personality and, as it were, no longer belonged to the earth but to the sky-world.

It does not seem that all men went through this ceremony, and, in any case, it did not make a man a karadji, or clever man. To reach this degree, the postulant had "to pass through water." He was thrown into a *nambi* (sacred waterhole) by other karadji, or else threw himself into it. Such water was endowed with life-giving and curative properties. Sick persons would be cured by being put through it. While in the water, the postulant looked up to Gulambrá, the sky cult-hero, and asked for power. Having brought him out of this life-giving water, the other karadji restored him to normal consciousness by laying their hands on his shoulders. During a further sojourn in the bush, he was given quartz stones to swallow, which he would later project when performing sorcery. He also acquired an individual totem *tjirkun*, which would henceforth help him in his profession.

As a result of his making, the karadji could go up to the sky in a dream, work evil magic, cure sick people, and influence people at a distance. He could "think strong." The curative process sometimes included catching and restoring the spirit of the sick man.[18]

The Clarence River doctors were made by sleeping on the grave of a deceased person.[19] The medicine men of the Kumbaingeri (Coombangree), a Bellinger River tribe, went to the mountains at set seasons of the year. While they fasted and endured privations there for months, "wild stones" (quartz crystals) were placed in their insides by Ulitarra (the first man, who became their god). The large rock crystal is the symbol of their Great Spirit.[20] Kumbaingeri medicine men can see the spirit of a murderer hanging around the corpse of his victim and, by the performance of a rite, can kill his spirit, which means, of course, causing him to be ill. Three medicine men are required to do this. They can also ascertain the name of the murderer by questioning the corpse on the way to burial.[21]

The Western Districts of New South Wales

The Wiimbaio medicine man was made by another one of the profession. The method included the procuring of the body of a dead man, the bones of which were pounded up and chewed. A state of frenzy was thus induced. Cannibalism was practiced in this tribe. If the men caught any person of another tribe whom they suspected of magical intentions, they killed him and ate part of his body. Bulmer, however, says there was no sign of cannibalism, though the Wiimbaio did, by way of revenge, take out the enemy's kidney fat, which they used for anointing themselves and for various magical purposes. The Wiimbaio doctors also used quartz crystals for magic.[22]

We have no information about the making of the Ta-ta-thi medicine men, but we are told that some of them obtained a special privilege of being carried aloft by the ghost of a woman. A medicine man invoked her powers by chewing a piece of skin that he had cut from her stomach after death and cured in the smoke of his campfire. He was thus able to visit the world of the sky, that being a solid vault, with a window that was guarded by a ghost.[23]

Beveridge says that a medicine man of the Laitu-laitu tribe was made by sleeping for a month in the hut built over the grave of a medicine man. He adds that it was usually the greatest scamp who was the candidate. One of the medicine man's privileges was that he could with safety see a spirit called Konikatine, who dwelt in the profound depths of the lakes, waterholes, and rivers. The doctor professed to go to the bottom of the river to him for days. He returned from his supposed visit with his eyes bloodshot and his cloak covered with ooze and gave accounts of his experiences. This descent was most likely part of the initiation, as well as henceforth a privilege and necessity, and represents the period of seclusion in which powers were given.[24] Laitu-laitu medicine men made rain by cutting off some of their own hair, oiling it with the kidney fat of some victim, placing it in the river, and speaking to a good spirit named Ngoudenout. Konikatine was supposed to guard the camp against the kidney-fat stealer. The medicine men were the only people who had seen spirits.[25]

We have no account of the making in the Bangerang tribe, but the taking of fat was practiced, presumably by medicine men. Curr says that "by means of a person's lock of hair, or remains of any of his food, and certain mysterious ceremonies, his caul-fat was surreptitiously extracted, when it was believed he either pined away or died" or met some fatal accident.[26]

Medicine men of the Wiradjeri were trained by their fathers,[27] but they had to go to Baiame, "the sky-god," for their powers. The following are the main features of the experience, as described by one postulant: Quartz crystals were rubbed into his body when he was a small boy and were also put into water for him to drink. As a result, he could see ghosts. After his initiation he was given power to bring up crystals, a necessary part of the doctor's equipment. After this he was taken into a grave, where he saw a dead man; the latter rubbed him all over to make him clever, and gave him some quartz crystals. He was then shown a tiger snake, to the tail of which a string was tied, such as the doctors bring up out of themselves. It was to be his secret totem, as it was his father's, who was initiating him. Taking hold of the string, he and his father were led by the snake into a hollow tree, in which were a lot of little Daramulans, the sons of Baiame, and then on into a hole full of snakes, which did not hurt him but rubbed themselves against him to make him clever. His father next took him up to Baiame's camp on a thread. They entered the sky through a place used by the medicine men. They saw Baiame, a very great old man, with a long beard, sitting in his camp with his legs under him. Two great quartz crystals extended from his shoulders to the sky above him.[28] There they found numbers of Baiame's boys and of his people, who are birds and beasts. It would seem that in becoming medicine men, they also became Baiame's people, for among their claims was that of entering into birds and beasts, as well as of turning themselves into inanimate objects and of walking invisibly.[29]

In 1943 I asked R. M. Berndt, who was doing research in the southwest of New South Wales for the Australian National Research Council, to see if there were any knowledgeable men, if not medicine men, at Menindee. He fortunately found two reliable informants who had been brought up by medicine men. They were not themselves doctors but were familiar with the powers and claims of the clever fellows and with the beliefs regarding them. The information gained corroborates and adds to what had been recorded by Howitt and Cameron. I give a summary of it here:

A postulant must have shown from his earliest years leanings toward the profession and have been in close association with a doctor, preferably his father or father's father, who was willing to train him and to impart to him some of his knowledge. Special sentences were constructed and used when talking to such a boy to test his powers and interpretation. Secrecy was impressed upon him, and the simpler aspects of the profession were revealed to him. He grew in magical power, as well as in knowledge. For example, the doctor's spirit would take the child's spirit away with him at night, even up to the sky, when he climbed there on a cord to make rain.

When the lad was about ten or twelve years of age, the doctor sang into him the assistant-totem (spirit companion or the "meat" [totem] within him). To do this, he chanted softly, and taking a little opossum from the air, he placed it on the lad's chest, or on some other part of his body, into which it sank. This totem was patrilineal, which was associated with the fact that the initiating doctor was the postulant's father or father's father. Actually the latter's assistant-totem caused itself to be doubled, so that it remained in the doctor at the same time as it materialized in the air and was transmitted into the youth. The postulant was taught the methods of using it and the song and ritual concentration necessary to release it from his body.

By the time the youth had been initiated into full tribal membership, he already knew some of the fundamental principles of this future profession, but he did not possess the power, insight, or control to work magic. This was to be given later in a ritual and spiritual experience.

When the young man was between twenty and thirty years of age, Baiame, the sky cult-hero, intimated in a dream to the postulant's teacher or guardian that he would receive him for the making. Similar dreams occurred to other guardians in the same or adjacent tribes. They all met at a fixed time with their candidates at a sacred place. The latter were seated on a long couch of leaves, while the doctors sang to summon Baiame. He came from out of the air toward the seated group. He looked like any doctor, except for the light that radiated from his eyes.

Coming up to each postulant, he said, "I'll make you," and caused sacred powerful water, called *kali* and said to be liquified quartz, to fall on him. This rite was called *kurini*, "the going into them." The water spread all over the postulant and was completely absorbed. Then feathers emerged from the latter's arms, which grew into wings in the course of two days. In the meantime, Baiame had gone, and the postulants were taught the significance of the water and the feathers. They ate sparingly.

In the next stage, each young man was sent off to meet Baiame, who, taking him to a special place, taught him how to fly and how to use quartz. Baiame sang a piece into his forehead so that he would be able to see right into things. He also took from his own body a flame, which he sang into the postulant's chest, and taught the postulant how he could release it. Then, directed back to his camp, he flew, sang off his wings, walked in, and sat alongside his guardian, with whom he discussed his experience.

The third experience occurred after all the postulants had been made. They went to the first sacred place and lay again on a couch of leaves. After the singing, Baiame appeared, placed a cord in "U" fashion across the chest and down the legs of each of them, and sang it into them. Henceforward, this was to be used as a spider uses his web. Baiame then bid them farewell and went away.

The young men, now doctors, remained in seclusion for two or three days practicing magical displays.

According to another account given by R. M. Berndt of the making of a doctor, the experience may come at a time or place without any pre-arranging or conditioning. In this case, a man who had been trained by his father in the necessary esoteric lore had come to the end of a successful day's hunting when he started to dig out an iguana. But he found himself dragged down and across to a strange country on the other side of the sea. Then Baiame carried him off to a very large cave, where he pierced him with his "X-ray" eyes and, looking into his mind, asked whether he had been made a man and also prepared by his father to receive Baiame's power and knowledge. On receiving an affirmative answer, Baiame "made a man of him again" and then made him a doctor in the way already described by Berndt's informants for the pre-arranged group making. The doctor concerned was said to be a Kamilaroi man from Brewarrina, but the method was the same as in the Wiradjeri.

A comparison of the description given by Howitt with these two recorded in 1943 by Berndt suggests that the former had for the most part been told only the preliminary though important and significant preparation of the postulant by his guardian or teacher, usually his father or father's father. It consisted of being

1. tested and entrusted with some esoteric knowledge,
2. endowed with an assistant-totem (also the father's),
3. taken to the sky on the doctor's cord.

Apparently, too, when Howitt's informant related that his father had caused quartz crystals to enter into him when he was a small boy, he was referring to his father's preliminary selection and magical preparation of him for his future career. The experience of being led into the tree and down into a great hole that occurred immediately after an initiation ceremony, and being shown his assistant-totem, was probably a hypnotic and magical display, such as the doctors or clever men of this tribe gave on the occasions of initiation.

One problem of interest is whether the later ritual of making by Baiame was mainly a trance experience and a materialization of what one had been taught to expect, or whether a doctor acted the part of Baiame. Probably both were true.

An outstanding feature in the making is the use of quartz, even in liquid form; it gives the doctor power to see right into a person's mind, and to fly. It is closely associated with Baiame in the sky and with the spirits of the dead. The putting of the flame and the cord into the postulant's body equips him for his future activities of causing fire to run along cords produced from his body, or of traveling in a "pillar" of fire that does not burn anything. He can also send the cord out of his body up to the sky or the top of a tree and climb up on it.

The Wiradjeri medicine men practice not only the usual bone-pointing and contagious magic but also a speical pointing in which use is made of the hair and fat of a dead man, whose spirit is supposed to help the charm to act. This suggests the taking of fat by the doctors, but the Wiradjeri gave Howitt the impression that it was only practiced by the doctors of tribes farther down the Murray and Murrumbidgee rather than by their own doctors.[30] Recent inquiry, however, reveals that the latter did take fat, extracting it through an elongated incision below the last rib on the rights side.[31]

Wiradjeri medicine men are also associated with Wawi, a serpentlike creature who lives in deep waterholes and burrows into the bank, where he makes his den. His wife and children live near. A medicine man wishing to see him paints himself first with red ochre and, after a rain, follows the rainbow, the end of which rests over the waterhole. He dives under the bank and finds Wawi, who takes him to his den and sings him a new corroboree, which he brings back to the clever men of the tribe. Wawi has the magical power of varying his size from 7 or 8 centimeters to prodigious proportions. The black streak in the Milky Way near the Southern Cross is one of his ancestors.[32]

In the neighboring tribe, the Wongaibon, between the Lachlan and the Darling, it is the personal totem that enables the medicine man to perform magic, and he therefore has one or more. Professor A. R. Brown, who gathered this information, could not ascertain how the totem was acquired. A. L. P. Cameron says that the Wongaibon doctor, *walmera,* is believed to acquire his powers either by being trained from boyhood by his father or by being instructed by the spirits of the dead.[33] The Murawari medicine man kept within his body an animal of the species that was his personal totem. He could produce it at will and send it to work magic.[34] Knowing now that the medicine-man rites and beliefs in the Wiradjeri, Wongaibon, and Murawari tribes are similar and, indeed, that the making might be a combined ceremony, we can infer that this information for the Wongaibon and Murawari must be supplemented by that given above for the Wiradjeri. According to Cameron, the doctors in this region could visit the sky-land, where they would go after death. In one case, a doctor sucked some dried skin and fat from a human corpse, the ghost of which took him up and through a hole in the sky-vault. There he gained valuable information, after which he was made to return. This refers to a Ta-ta-thi doctor, but Cameron says it is typical.[35]

We have very little information for the rest of the west of New South Wales, with the exception of the Yualai. The Barkinji medicine man showed his power by sucking from a victim a *yountoo* (dead man's bone) or a *moolee* (a piece of quartz) that had been pointed at him. The ritual of pointing either of these missiles, which included the flesh and fat respectively of a dead body, was so complicated that only a specially trained person could perform it. He was probably a type of doctor, especially as a moolee, a rough piece of white quartz with a piece of twine fastened at one end, gave its possessor aid in composing new corroborees.[36] The office in the Tongaranka tribe passed from father to son, but the latter only practiced on the death of the former. The medicine men of this and the other tribes of the Itchumundi nation used the fibula of a dead man for pointing.[37] Newland says that an old Wampangee medicine man explained how he visited "heaven" when young. It was part of his making. He was taught the lore by an old medicine man, whose powers, on his death, descended to his pupil. The old man had instructed the latter to cut out and eat a piece of the flesh of his thigh as soon as he died. The young man did this, and his spirit flew at once to a place beyond the sky, where he saw the "goddess and the lesser female divinities" and good fruits and general plenty.[38] In the Kamiliaroi tribe, the office was hereditary, and the practitioners could throw and extract stones. During an initiation in the most northern part of the tribe, the medicine men produced white stones and other substances, and one of them drank human blood. One observer (the Reverend C. C. Greenway) says that men could acquire magical or supernatural power, and refers to the use of magical stones and cords.[39]

Yualai (Euahlayi) medicine men select a boy who is to follow their profession. They take him to a tribal burial ground at night, tie him down, and after having lit some fires of fat (not stated if human) at short distances around him, leave him there. The following is an account of one man's experiences when so left: A spirit came, turned him over, and went. A big star fell beside him, and from it came an iguana (his totem), which ran all over him and then went away. After this, a snake, the hereditary enemy of the iguana, crawled on him, frightening him. Next a huge figure came and drove a yam-stick right through his head, placing in the hole a sacred stone, with the help of which much of the initiate's magic in the future was to be worked. Then "came the spirits of the dead, who corroboreed around him, chanting songs full of sacred lore as regards the art of healing and instructions how, when he needed it, he could call upon their aid." He was released next day by a wizard but was tied down again at night—this time on a bower bird's playground, where he was again visited by spirits of the dead and taught more lore. The bower bird, before being changed into a bird, was a great medicine man. Finally, the postulant was tied down for several nights in case he should be frightened. He was kept away from his camp for about two months and was not allowed to become a practitioner until he was some years older.

The sacred stones, such as the one that was placed in the head of the novice referred to, are said to be about the size and shape of a small lemon and like a lump of semitransparent crystal. Those who have the most stones are the most powerful medicine men, and there is often a great rivalry at tribal meetings to see which wizard can produce the most. "The strength of the stone in them, whether swallowed or rubbed in through their heads, adds its strength to theirs, for these stones are living spirits, as it were, breathing and growing in their fleshly cases, the owner having power to produce them at any time. The dying bequeath their stones to living *wireenuns* [medicine men] most nearly related to them." It is in such stones that the cleverest medicine men see visions of the past, of what is happening in the present at a distance, and of the future. They can cause instant death by directing rays from these stones toward their victims. The spirit is said to go out of the crystal gazing stone to the person of whom knowledge is sought and to show that person in the crystal.[40]

Quartz crystals and medicine men are associated with the sky-world and with Baiame, the sky culture-giver. Only medicine men are allowed to hold intercourse with him, and then only through his spirit messenger. Baiame is fixed to the crystal rock on which he sits. In order to get in touch with him, the medicine men have to descend the mountain Oobi-oobi, beyond the top of which lies Baiame's sky-home. Once when they wanted the earth to be made beautiful again after a drought, they did this in the following manner: Coming to the mountain, they found foot-holes cut in the rocks, making a ladder. After four days, they reached the top, where they saw a stone excavation, into which bubbled up a spring of fresh water. From this they drank thirstily and found it so invigorated them as to make them lose all feeling of tiredness. They saw circles of piled-up stones a little distance from the spring. Going into one of these, they heard almost immediately the sound of *gayandi*, the medium through which the voice of Baiame's spirit-messenger was heard.[41] Having made their requests, they were lifted by some of the attendant spirits of the sacred mountain through the sky to Baiame's land. They were told to gather all the blossoms they could, after which they were brought back to the mountain and returned to their tribe.[42]

Some members of the Yualai tribe, principally medicine

men, or men intended to be such, have not only totems and sub- (or multiplex) totems, but also individual totems, called *yunbeai,* which they must never eat or else they will die. Any injury to this totem hurts the person. "In danger, he has the power to assume the shape of his yunbeai, which, of course, is of great assistance to him. Further, an individual has a *Minggah,* or spirit-haunted tree, which is usually chosen from among his multiplex totems. But the very greatest wizards, and they only, have instead spirit-haunted stones, which are called *Goomah.* A person's yunbeai may be kept there, and spirits friendly toward the person whose Minggah or Goomah it is, dwell there. If a wizard needs such help as can be obtained from the spirits dwelling at his Minggah or Goomah, he either goes to them or else sends his dream spirit to interview them. His dream spirit is different from that of ordinary people and bears a different name. He has complete control over it, but they have not over theirs. These spirit-animated trees and stones are places of refuge in time of danger, but the latter type possess the greater sanctity. Not even a medicine man would touch a refugee at one of these stones, while at the former, the wizard whose Minggah it was could interfere." Mrs. Parker's account suggests that such centers are connected only with medicine men.[43]

Each individual Yualai has three, or perhaps four, spirits, one of which is his shadow-spirit. Here we meet with the special sanctity of the medicine man: his shadow, like his head, is taboo. Anyone touching it will be made to suffer for such sacrilege.

In addition to consulting spirits for their own purposes and practicing crystal gazing, the Yualai medicine men hold mediumistic meetings at which other persons can be present.

One of the special powers of the medicine man is to use a pointing-stick to the end of which is tied some hair taken from the intended victim's head.

In August-September 1944, while engaged in work among the Aborigines, mostly of mixed blood, in Weilwan and Kamilaroi country, I met one clever man, or *wiringin,* to use the Weilwan term, and also several persons who had known wiringin, knew something of their making, and believed in their powers. The ritual was similar to that in the Wiradjeri, Yualai, and Wongaibon tribes.

One or more wiringin took the aspirant to the vicinity of a burial place or a ghost place in the bush and instructed him to lie down there, usually covered with bark. A fire of fat was lit nearby, and the novice was instructed to lie still, keep his eyes slightly open, and not be frightened even though a big snake crawled on him. This snake, or some other creature, would be his assistant-totem, or familiar, his "spirit." The doctors then went some distance away and watched. When the snake came, the aspirant was told to pat it and not flinch. After this, the supreme test occurred. A ghost, like a skeleton, or resembling a white corpse, appeared, usually coming down from a tree. I met two men and was told of four others who fled in terror at the sight of the spirit. One of those who failed thought that the two officiating doctors brought the ghost down. He had noticed that just before reaching the burial tree in the "cemetery," a blaze of fire went through the air toward the tree, a sign of a wiringin's power. Clear stones (*kabara*), magic cord, and a spirit-animal, or reptile, were put in the postulant.

Training followed this experience. The new doctor was taught how to diagnose and treat illness, to produce the magical stones and cord and his assistant-totem from his body, to summon the spirits, and to exercise various psychic powers. Years were required to become proficient in some parts of the craft, and some doctors were more clever than others. Among their powers were learning what was happening at a distance by sending their spirit-helpers to find out or by going oneself in spirit form, traveling at a speed exceeding any normal speeds, disappearing as though into the air, giving displays suggestive of conjuring and hypnotism, and walking through the fire unharmed. The retention of these powers depended on some degree of self-discipline. For example, one clever man has lost, through excessive drinking, the power to know in advance who is coming.[44]

The accounts indicate that the making and powers of medicine men were of one type among the tribes in the eastern part of the Darling River system: the Yualai, Kamilaroi, Weilwan, Wongaibon, and Wiradjeri, and possibly some of their neighbors, also. The initiates of the "high degree" of these tribes formed an esoteric brotherhood who shared a common knowledge and met occasionally, especially at intertribal gatherings, and whose knowledge was not questioned.

Eastern and Northern Queensland

Medicine men of the Chepara (Jagara) tribe (Brisbane district) could fly up to heaven to consult the supernatural being, Maamba, as the result of having swallowed some quartz crystal. They displayed a large crystal at initiation, which was said to come from Maamba. The power of the Turrbal medicine man, together with his quartz crystal, was handed down from father to son. The special pieces of quartz that the medicine men possessed were obtained from deep pools, creeks, and similar places, where they dived for it. Targan, the individual who was responsible for the rainbow, vomited them out and deposited them in such places. The medicine men knew where to dive for them, namely, where the rainbow ended. They were also supposed to send rain and squalls and to cut the rainbow off where it was held to the river bottom. With them he could dive into the ground and come out again where he liked. His spirit could take crystals through space and place them in a victim's body and so doom the latter. This dooming meant "being cut up into small pieces and being put together again." The medicine man could also fly through the air.[45]

The Kabi and Wakka called this rainbow being Dhakkan or Takkan. He was a combination of fish and snake and lived in the deepest waterholes. When visible as a rainbow, he was passing from one to another. He had a terrible side to his nature, for he could shatter trees and shrubs and slaughter men. A man with many crystals in his body could lie down to sleep on the margin of Dhakkan's watery dwelling. The prickly sensation caused through the cold and sluggish circulation was regarded as a sign that he had been taken to Dhakkan's domain, where he gave the spirit magic stones and received cord or crystals in return. Such a person would wake up full of life and be a medicine man of the highest degree. His power was associated with quartz crystals, in particular, a large white one, which were carried both in his insides and in his bag. He also used certain flat circular black stones, which were probably obsidianites. These stones and also some cord (*bukkur*) were bestowed on him by benevolent spirits inhabiting mineral springs.[46] The reference to a man having many stones in his insides before going down to Dhakkan for his endowment with power and life (*muru muru*, full of life) implies a preliminary stage in the doctor's progress.

The medicine men of Fraser Island can fly up like birds and go into the earth and come out again at a considerable distance. Further, they cannot be killed and will never die.[47] The office is hereditary on the Tully River, but nothing is known about the training. There are no special graduates at Cape Bedford, but certain old men assume the power of a medicine man and are described by the name of Danbun, a nature spirit identical with Aru-a, who teaches the practitioners of the Princess Charlotte Bay tribe. The Pennefather River medicine men are said to learn their business at the graveside from the spirits of deceased persons. When they go away for a spell in the bush, they are believed to talk to the spirits, with whose assistance they control people's lives.[48]

Speaking generally of the north Queensland tribes, Roth says that "many of the nature spirits are originally derived from the bodies of dead people, that is, from spirits that have, taken to the solitudes of the mountain or forest." The medicine men can insert and withdraw the usual magical substances, including quartz crystals, "with which their graduation or reputation is so intimately associated." They can control the forces of nature. In addition to deriving assistance occasionally from the dead and from nature spirits, they can also obtain it from the blood of their victims. Thus, among the Kungganji of Cape Grafton "the medicine men used to doom their victims by choking them during sleep, piercing the head with a bone-splinter plunged just above each nostril, taking out the tongue and removing the life-blood." This blood had the property of enabling the medicine men who drank it to fly over immense stretches of country.[49]

In the Maikulan (Mycoolan) tribe, to the southeast of the Gulf of Carpentaria, the principal old men, or medicine men, have charge of a particular kind of crystal, called *rore,* which is regarded as being in some way connected with their future existence. Such crystals are obtained from natives' insides by medicine men or, with some ceremony and much privation, in the mountain districts. The spirits of the dead, whose home is among the stars, show themselves to medicine men.[50]

Yir-Yoront medicine men learn or inherit their art from a relative. In this tribe, sorcerers remove kidney fat and other vital parts with a pointing-bone type of instrument and send poison snakes and crocodiles to destroy their victims. The sorcerers, like the medicine men, learn their art from a relative. It includes control of occult powers.[51]

The Southwestern Corner (Western Australia)

We have little evidence for the narrow uncircumcised strip of Western Australia. The medicine men of New Norcia had the usual powers. These reside in certain little stones, a kind of quartz, in their stomachs, which passed at death into the stomachs of their sons.[52] Referring to a larger area that included New Norcia, Grey says that the natives of the southwest of Australia paid a respect, almost amounting to veneration, to shining stones or pieces of crystal, which they called Teyl, and which none but the sorcerers were allowed to touch.[53] The medicine men were supposed to be able to transport themselves through the air at pleasure and to render themselves invisible to all but others of the profession. They could hear everything and could consume a person's flesh but not his bones. Mrs. Bates says that the office was not hereditary in the south, but that it was in the Gascoyne and Ashburton districts, though even there it was claimed that a man could make himself a medicine man, with power to hold communion with a mythical snake named Kajoora. Crystals were used as elsewhere.[54]

Notes

1. Taplin, "The Narrinyeri," in Woods, *Native Tribes*, pp. 23–31, for forms of sorcery, and p. 46 for deprecatory reference to doctors. H. E. A. Meyer, "The Encounter Bay Tribe," in Woods, pp. 195–97. Taplin (ibid., p. 29) said that the Narrinyeri abhorred the horrible practice of the upper river (Murray) tribes of extracting the kidney-fat of their living enemies.
2. James Dawson, *Australian Aborigines* (Melbourne: G. Robertson, 1881), pp. 55–58.
3. Howitt, *Native Tribes*, pp. 368–71, 414–440, 489, 490, 433. He comments that these tribes seem to have kept to themselves certain beliefs concerning their sky-being. Moreover, they had no initiation ceremonies of the general Eastern type, in which the beliefs about the sky-world and sacred objects were disclosed, p. 491. Howitt puts the Jupagalk on the east of the Wotjobaluk, p. 55.
4. Ibid., pp. 393, 404, 438. Howitt thinks that the Wotjo also put the home of

the dead in the sky. *Kulin* is the word for man among several Victorian tribes, p. 70.

5. Ibid., p. 405. Compare Howitt, *Journal of the Royal Anthropological Institute* 13:185, 186, 188.
6. That is, the extraction of kidney- or caul-fat from a human victim without leaving a mark, death ensuing about three days later.
7. Howitt, *Native Tribes*, pp. 365, 375, 381, 405, 435, 436, 491. The dual organization is the division of the tribe into two social and ceremonial divisions, which are unilateral in descent and usually exogamous. See Elkin, *Australian Aborigines*, pp. 121–24.
8. Howitt, *Native Tribes*, pp. 73, 389, 399.
9. This is a rounded and generally black pebble, which the medicine man carried about and occasionally showed to people as a threat. Howitt, *Native Tribes*, p. 378.
10. Medicine men were taken to the sky on a sort of rope, sometimes said to be like steps. One informant spoke of it as a road along which the dead went to the sky. Howitt, *Journal of the Royal Anthropological Institute* 13:196.
11. Howitt, *Native Tribes*, pp. 408–9. In the Kurnai burial ritual, the "bundle" of bones, which had been carried about for a long time, was finally put up in a tree. Ibid., p. 459.
12. Howitt, *Journal of the Royal Anthropological Institute* 13:186.
13. Howitt, *Native Tribes*, pp. 361, 372, 378.
14. Ibid., p. 485. Brough Smyth, *The Aborigines of Victoria*, vol. 1, pp. 453–455.
15. Howitt, *Native Tribes*, pp. 373, 376, 405, 437, 523. The home of the dead is in the sky, according to the beliefs of these tribes.
16. D. Collins, *An Account of the English Colony in New South Wales* (London: T. Cadell and W. Davies, 1798–1802), p. 383. Howitt, *Native Tribes*, p. 405. L. Threlkeld, "An Australian Grammar" in J. Fraser, *An Australian Language* (Sydney: Sydney Government Printer, 1892), p. 48. Threlkeld states that in the Awabakal language (near Lake Macquarie) *Morrokum* is a magical bone, which is inserted into the thighs of each of three doctors by the spirit of the recently interred person. They sleep on his grave, after which they can cause death by making the bone enter the body of their victim.
17. Howitt, *Native Tribes*, pp. 376, 383.
18. Elkin, Field Notes.
19. G. F. Angas, *Savage Life and Scenes in Australia and New Zealand* (London: Smith Elder, 1847), vol 2, p. 233.
20. A. C. McDougall, "Manners, Customs and Legends of the Coombangree Tribe," *Science of Man* 3:117. E. Palmer, "Notes on Some Australian Tribes," *Journal of the Royal Anthropological Institute* 13: 296–97. Palmer refers to the "headman" or doctor or spirit-medium.
21. Elkin, Field Notes. An informant told me in 1936 that he had seen magical

cord produced from a doctor's mouth. He also said that during the period of seclusion and training a large snake crawled over the postulant and put magical things in him.

22. Howitt, *Native Tribes*, pp. 366–67, 404. J. Bulmer, "Some Account of the Aborigines of the Lower Murray, Wimmera, Gippsland and Maneroo," *Victorian Geographical Journal* 5:16–18. Howitt, *Native Tribes*, p. 367, gives an interesting account of the method of extraction, but it was credited to the men of hostile tribes. It seems to have been useful for blacks to ascribe to hostile tribes such practices as cannibalism and fat-taking, which they felt met with the disapproval of white people. Wiimbaio are the same people as the Maraura. See N. B. Tindale, "Distribution of Australian Aboriginal Tribes," *Transactions of the Royal Society*, S. A., 64:192.
23. Howitt, *Native Tribes*, p. 389; *Journal of the Royal Anthropological Institute* 13:197.
24. Compare the Brisbane medicine men, who dived to the bottom of deep pools to obtain their magical quartz, which was associated with the rainbow. Roth, *Superstition, Magic*, p. 30.
25. P. Beveridge, *The Aborigines of Victoria and the Riverina* (Melbourne: M. L. Hutchinson, 1889), pp. 64, 96–97, 99–100. Beveridge refers to the Aborigines of Victoria and Riverina, apparently the Laitu-laitu. A. R. Brown, "Notes on the Social Organization of Australian Tribes," *Journal of the Royal Anthropological Institute* 48 (1918): 249.
26. E. M. Curr, *Recollections of Squatting in Victoria* (Melbourne: George Robertson, 1883), p. 276. The mention of mysterious ceremonies suggested that the fat-taking was practiced by a specially trained person, such as a medicine man.
27. The office was apparently hereditary. Later research has shown that this was so.
28. There was, apparently, a sky above the sky-world.
29. Howitt, *Native Tribes*, pp. 374, 405–8.
30. Ibid., pp. 360, 361, 373, 374. The Murrumbidgee Aborigines sometimes come over to the Lachlan River by night and, if possible, kill some natives and take their fat. S. C. R. Bowler, "Aboriginal Customs," *Science of Man* 4:203. See also A. L. P. Cameron, "Notes on Some Tribes of New South Wales," *Journal of the Royal Anthropological Institute* 14 (1885):361.
31. R. M. Berndt, "Wuradjeri Magic and Clever Men," p. 72. The wound was, as usual, closed up without leaving a mark, and the victim became ill two or three days later. The doctor might extract this fat while in a trance, sending out his assistant-totem in its spirit form, traveling in a whirlwind to seek the victim and to operate on him.
32. R. H. Mathews, *Ethnological Notes on the Aboriginal Tribes of New South Wales and Victoria* (Sydney: F. W. White, Printer, 1905), p. 162.

33. Brown, "Notes on the Social Organization," p. 432. Cameron, "Some Tribes of NSW," p. 360. Wongaibon *walmera* is *walemira* in Wiradjeri.
34. Brown, "Notes on Social Organization," p. 442.
35. Cameron, "Some Tribes of NSW," pp. 360–61.
36. C. Bonney, "On Some Customs of the Aborigines of the River Darling," *Journal of the Royal Anthropological Institute* 13 (1884): 130. Fat extraction was undoubtedly one of his powers. Mourning was ended by the taking of the sorcerer's caul-fat. E. M. Curr, *The Australian Race* (Melbourne: J. Ferres, Government Printer, 1886–87), vol. 2, p. 199.
37. Howitt, *Native Tribes*, pp. 360, 404.
38. S. Newland, "The Parkengees or Aboriginal Tribes on the Darling River," *South Australian Geographical Journal* 2 (1887–88): 31. He includes the Wampangee in the Barkinji community, p. 20. This agrees with G. N. Teulon in Curr, *Australian Race*, vol. 2, p. 189. See also Howitt, *Native Tribes*, p. 50, and R. H. Mathews, "The Group Divisions and Initiation Ceremonies of the Barkunjee Tribes," *Royal Society of NSW* 32:241.
39. Ridley, *Kamilaroi*, p. 158. R. H. Mathews, "The Bora of the Kamilaroi Tribes," *Royal Society of Victoria* 9 (1896): 167. Greenway, "Australian Languages and Traditions," pp. 242–43. Fat extraction was practiced. Howitt, *Native Tribes*, p. 376.
40. Parker, *Euahlayi Tribe*, pp. 25–27, 35–36.
41. Medicine men had to enter one of these circles on the mountain if they desired an interview with the messenger. K. L. Parker, *More Australian Legendary Tales* (London: Nutt, 1898), p. 90. The sound of Gayandi is the noise of the bull-roarer.
42. Parker, *More Australian Legendary Tales*, pp. 84–92. The dead initiated men also go up to the sky-world by way of this mountain. Parker, *Euahlayi Tribe*, pp. 90–91.
43. Parker, *Euahlayi Tribe*, pp. 20–21, 27–29, 35–36. Compare the sacred storehouses of the central tribes, which are also places of refuge. Spencer and Gillen, *Native Tribes*, p. 135.
44. Howitt, *Native Tribes*, p. 409, quotes a similar case of the loss of magical power through drinking—a doctor of the Kurnai tribe.
45. Roth, *Superstition, Magic*, p. 30. Howitt, *Native Tribes*, pp. 398, 581–82. A falling star was a medicine man flying through the air and dropping his firestick to kill someone, p. 429. Howitt, ibid., p. 86, puts the Turrbal immediately north of the Chepara but overlapping the latter. They were probably one tribe, the Jagara. Compare Tindale, map, in "Distribution in Australian Aboriginal Tribes," p. 176.
46. J. Mathew, *Two Representative Tribes of Queensland* (London: T. Fisher Unwin, 1910), pp. 170–72, 174–76.
47. E. Fuller in Curr, *Australian Race*, vol. 3, p. 147.

48. Roth, *Superstition, Magic,* pp. 18, 30.
49. Ibid., pp. 28, 29, 34.
50. E. Palmer, "Concerning Some Superstitions of North Queensland Aborigines," *Royal Society of Queensland* 2 (1885): 166–67, 171–72.
51. Sharp, "Ritual Life and Economics of the Yir-Yoront," pp. 35–36.
52. R. Salvado, *Mémoires historiques sur l'Australie, traduits de l'italien en francais par l'abbé Falsimagne* (Paris, 1854), p. 261.
53. G. Grey, *Journals of Two Expeditions of Discovery in Northwestern and Western Australia* (London: T. & W. Boone, 1841), vol. 2, pp. 337, 340.
54. D. Bates, "The Marriage Laws and Some Customs of the West Australian Aborigines," *Victorian Geographical Journal* 23 (1905): 57.

CHAPTER 4

The Circumcision Regions

South Australia and the Neighboring Region of Western Australia

Medicine men around Adelaide were associated with cannibalism in their making and with quartz in their practice. Aspirants had at one period to eat the flesh of young children and at another that of an old man, though it does not appear that they partook more than once in their lives of each kind. "They have sacred implements or relics which are for the most part carefully concealed from the eyes of all, but especially from the women, such as pieces of rock crystal, said to have been extracted by them from individuals said to be suffering from the withering influence of some hostile sorcerers."[1] The Narrang-ga medicine men could commune with the departed spirits and receive power from them to inflict evil magic by songs, but they could also work cures. The position was said to be hereditary.[2] The Pankala (Parnkalla) medicine men had a special place after death, called heaven's cavern. Their names seem to have been mentioned after death, whereas the names of other people were taboo for a considerable period after their decease. The office was hereditary.[3] The medicine men of the Yerkla-Mining are said to be the headmen.[4] The Wirangu (at the head of the Great Australian Bight) say that a postulant is swallowed by Djidara, a large snake whose tracks are Lakes Gairdner, Torrens, and others, and after having passed through this creature's insides, becomes a medicine man. The practitioners use shining substances such as *karar* (pearl-shell).[5]

The tribes of the western desert of South Australia gathered around Ooldea in 1941–42 may be considered as one cultural group, because of the fundamental unity of their language, social organization, totemism, and mythology. Among them, the *kinkin* (doctor) is also said to be a clever man. Like other individuals in the tribe, he can practice sorcery, but he is also a healer (*nangaringu,* one who sucks out), a rain-maker, an oracle, and a diviner of the cause of deaths. As well, he can counteract alien magical influences and can send his spirit in the form of his cult-totem to gather information from a distance.

The ritual and experience of the making take place at Djabudi waterhole, southwest of Ooldea, which is associated with a great snake, Wonambi, who is alive today, even though his mythical exploits belong to the ancestral dreamtime. He is the guardian of all doctors.

1. The postulant, who must have shown leanings toward the profession at an early age, goes to Djabudi accompanied only by kinkin. He is mourned for as a person just dead, because he is going to be *daramara,* that is, "cut into pieces," but signifying that he is to receive power. At Djabudi, he is blindfolded with a hair girdle by two doctors and given to the monstrous snake, which swallows him whole.
2. After the postulant has spent an undefined period of

seclusion inside the snake, the two doctors, who have been camped nearby, give the snake two kangaroo rats, in return for which he ejects the postulant into the air so that he falls alongside a certain rock hole.

3. A little later, the doctors begin a journey of search for the postulant, visiting and camping at each of a series of rock holes until they find him at the last one. But he has become a baby, Wonambi having made him like that. Taking him in their arms, they fly back to their camp.
4. Here songs are sung and ceremonies performed by a group of doctors, who have gathered from adjacent "countries." The postulant is placed within a circle of fires, and, as a result, he grows and attains again man's size. He then announces that he knows Wonambi, having been inside his stomach. He and Wonambi are friends.
5. He next begins a period of seclusion, during which he meditates and has converse with spirits. At the end of this, doctors take him into the bush and red-ochre him completely. He is made to lie full-length on his back before fires and is said to be a dead man. The head doctor proceeds to break his neck and his wrists and to dislocate the joints at the elbows, the upper thighs, the knees and ankles. A black stone, a charmed australite, is used to "cut" the above parts of the body in this daramara rite. Actually, the operator does not amputate each part properly, but rather makes a mark with the stone. It is interesting to notice that before the "cutting," the postulant's limbs are taut like those of a corpse, but at the touch of the doctor they become limp. This reviving of the limb is connected with the fact that the doctor puts into each cut a *maban* shell of life-giving properties. Maban are also put into his ears and into the angle of his jaw, so that he can respectively hear (understand) and speak to everything—spirits, strangers, and birds and animals; into his fore-

head, so that he can divine and see through anything; and into his neck, so that it may be turned in all directions. His stomach is also filled with maban in order that he may have renewed life and become invulnerable to attack by any weapon. He is then sung by the kinkin and revives. After this, all return to the main camp.

6. On arrival there, a test is held. All the fully initiated men, when ordered by the head kinkin, thrust and throw their spears at the *aringbulga,* as the postulant is now called. But the spears glance off because he is full of maban. He is now a kinkin and can practice his profession.

This is a remarkable but not unexpected ritual pattern. It consists of

1. the postulant being swallowed by a mythical snake and reborn as a child;
2. a fire ceremony and growth or restoration of the postulant to adult size; and
3. the treatment of the postulant as a corpse, which is ritually cut into pieces, each piece or part being made to live by the introduction of a magical life-giving substance; indeed, the cutting with the charmed stone-knife is a life-giving act.

The new life, so gained, is on a higher plane than the former one; the new doctor can see, hear, and say anything and is invulnerable. No one concerned has any doubt that this sequence of events occurs; nor need we have any doubts; some do occur in ritual and symbolic action, and some while in a state of trance.[6]

When I was in the Musgrave Ranges, northern South Australia, in 1930, an informant told me about a big waterhole in the country of the Pitjintara (Pidjindara) tribe to the northwest, in which a big snake, Wonambi, lives. He is fed with kangaroos. Men going to visit this place are met by local men (that is, men of the local Wonambi cult-totem), who blindfold them and throw them into the snake's mouth. They are swallowed, kept inside for four days, and then vomited out. After this, they must remain four days getting rabbits and other food for Wonambi. Men who have had this experience have permanent red piebald "markings on their backs."

This is probably an exoteric and garbled account of the making of medicine men or else of a totemic rite that is performed from time to time at this waterhole. Some weeks later, and 320 kilometers east, I was shown a stone tjurunga (totemic symbol), the markings on which depicted the tracks of Wonambi. It belonged to a man whose cult-totem was Wonambi.

I also heard of Wonambi in the Laverton district of Western Australia toward the end of 1930, and in addition recorded an interesting, though brief, account of the making of medicine men. The latter referred to the Mandjindja tribe out Warburton Range way. Wonambi is a cult-totem and, as well as dwelling in certain sacred sites, appears in dreams. If a woman dreams that she kills and eats Wonambi snake, she will bear a child whose conception totem will be Wonambi. At one waterhole, Kolornga, the Wonambi is 36 meters long and 1 meter thick. At another place, Kadada, Wonambi stands up as tall as the sky and can fly to other places. Wonambi plays an important part in the mythology and cult-totemism of western South Australia and the adjoining region of Western Australia, which can be justly described as a great desert region. In such a region, where water is precious, a recognized function of the great snake, as the guardian of at least some special waterholes, is understandable. Wonambi takes the water away when he "smells a stranger."

The account of the making that I recorded for the Mandjindja contains no reference to Wonambi, and a cave takes the place of a waterhole in the rite. The postulant goes into a cave where *wega* (the wild cat), and *kalaia* (the emu)[7] "kill" him and cut him open from his neck down the front of his body to the groin. They take out his heart, intestines, and other organs and insert *marbain* (magical substances). They take out his shoulder bones, cut along the thighs and take out the thigh bones. They dry the bones and, before putting them back, insert marbain. They cut round the ankles and stuff marbain into those parts. Finally, they take the frontal bone out, clean it, and insert marbain in the head before returning this bone to its place.

During the making, the head medicine man makes fires at night; he sleeps during the day. After the postulant has been duly provided with magic, he makes him get up and gives him blood to drink.

This head doctor has maban or marbain as his cult-totem. The totemic site is a stone cave in which a man, snakes, and marbain can be seen cut in the stone. The postulant goes to this cave and, after having given a present to the owner, is made to lie down and in due time comes out a medicine man. Possibly a trance is induced and the postulant believes that magical substances have been inserted in his body in the interesting way just described; or, what is most likely, two doctors play the part of the totemic heroes and ritually operate on him, making marks where the incisions and insertions would be made in an actual operation. He does drink human blood and also eats wild cat, porcupine, and emu.

A medicine man apparently has spirits of these species in his "mind," for he can send them into a sick man to take his sickness out of him. Sometimes he may send a spirit-child, *djidji,* instead.[8]

This account, which corresponds to stage 5 in the Ooldea description, is almost certainly incomplete. It is probable that Wonambi would come into the ritual at some point. He is associated with *kalaia* (an officiant) at some sacred waterholes (e.g., Kumbudji). But near Laverton, a great snake, there called *tarbidi*, protects the waterhole in the same way as Wonambi, and standing up like the rainbow (which he is), smells strangers. He is the supplier of shells, which can be found in the soak, and which he is said to bring there from under the sea in another country. In other words, he is associated with pearl-shell, or marbain, which is a source of power to the medicine man. The doctors of this area act as coroners, as well as healers.[9]

Referring to the eastern part of this Aluridja region, to the Kokata and the Antakerinya, formerly on the south and north of Oodnadatta respectively, we find that the doctor can see the spirit of a dead person hanging around the grave and is also able to catch hold of it and put it into a relative of the deceased (such as the widow or father) or into some other person, or into himself, where it stays, acting as a guardian or assistant-spirit. A doctor might have several of these spirits in him, and if he is called in to treat a sick person, he might send one of them to find and bring back the sick man's wandering spirit. Thus, the doctor has direct association with, and some control over, the spirits of the dead.

In northern South Australia, a medicine man (*nangari*) accompanies the revenge expedition, the members of which wear the "magical" *kadaitja* "shoes." After the victim has been speared, the nangari heats a white stone and puts it on the wound, causing it to heal without leaving a mark. He also puts a spirit-snake or something else of magical virtue in the victim's inside. Then starting the latter on the track that leads to his camp, he restores him to consciousness. The victim goes home as though nothing had occurred but sickens in two or three days. This suggests that, because of his own experience of having been killed, given magical insides, and raised, the medicine man can do the like to intended victims. The same pattern is used to endow with power or to kill. This principle is also obvious with regard to the making in the Aranda and other tribes.[10]

To pass to the northeastern region of South Australia: in the Ngaduri tribe in the middle north of that state, the postulant is singled out by medicine men when a child, because he acts in a grownup way. At puberty, unlike other growing boys, he avoids young women. After initiation, he goes into solitary seclusion, where he meditates, converses with spirits, goes into trances, and sees visions. During this period, when he is considered ritually dead, he receives his power. At the end of it, he is trained by other doctors. Until the age of thirty, he abstains from sexual intercourse.[11]

The Dieri medicine men (*kunki*) have direct communication with supernatural beings and spirits of the dead, called *kutji,* and also with the Mura-Muras, the mythological culture-heroes of the tribe. They interpret dreams, deciding which are victims caused by the kutji. They claim that like the latter, they can, by means of a hair-cord, go up to the beautiful sky-country, which is full of trees and birds, and drink its water, "from which they obtain the power to take the life of those they doom."[12]

The kunki also act as coroners. When doing so, they usually either question the corpse or see the murderer's spirit, unknown to himself, hanging around the grave or corpse. During dreams, the medicine man's spirit, sometimes in totemic guise, may visit distant persons, or be visited by them.[13]

The Dieri medicine man is made by the spirits, although a medicine man of his own totemic group may assist him. A young man who desires to be made must have shown great interest in tribal lore, a tendency to psychic experience, and an attachment to the elders and medicine men. One of the latter takes him into a bush place for a three-day period of seclusion. Here he meditates on the spiritual experience and powers about which he has been instructed, until the kutji, or spirit, being materialized, makes him. On the first day, he gives the postulant special food and, above all, changes his mind or way of thinking for that of a medicine man. The kunki then explain this experience to him.

On the second day, an incision is made by the spirit in the young man's stomach, into which a spirit-snake is inserted. This spirit-snake can be sent, during meditation, to obtain information for the medicine man. At some time or other, he visits the sky-world. A native doctor, in giving an account of his making, simply said that on the second day the spirit performed (rites) on him, and on the third day told him that he was now a proper kunki, and so now he would give him his equipment.[14]

One Dieri kunki related to Siebert that, when still a boy, he was made by being tied up, taken to the Ranges, and placed in a dark place, where a pointed stick was placed in the ground near him. He was asked whether he could see kutji, and when he answered no, he was told that he would see him. Later, when he was in seclusion, following on his circumcision, he suddenly saw a light going and coming near him. Terrified, he fled from the kutji. But now he was qualified to become a medicine man and was admitted into the mysteries by his father, a kunki.[15]

Obviously, the Dieri candidate is conditioned in body and mind for the traditional visionary experience. The spirit materializes and makes him; after this, he can be trained.

The only note I have for the Wailpi, of the Flinders Range on the south of the Dieri, is that the medicine man can see the spirits of the dead.

Among the Piladapa (neighbors of the Dieri), the kutji drives into the back of the would-be doctor's head a round stick, somewhat larger than a pencil, with a string fastened to one end. The postulant then opens his eyes. In other words, he has a vision of being pointed by the spirit and then gradually comes to. The spirit must always accompany a practitioner, for it is from the spirit that the *kunkikeri* obtains quartz and his power. If he has a serious grievance against a person, he kills the latter by extracting his heart, liver, and insides generally.[16]

North-Central Australia and Northwestern Queensland

Among the Arunta (Aranda), any man may employ sorcery, but the medicine men alone can counteract its effects. They can cure the sick, conduct inquests, accompany the kadaitja revenge expeditions (as described for northwestern South Australia), and act as mediums. Incidentally, dogs as well as medicine men can see spirits. Spencer and Gillen did not gather that the doctors claimed to travel through the air, though they were told that among some tribes, for example, the Mungaberra, west of the Macdonnell Ranges, doctors assume the form of eaglehawks, travel long distances by night to camps in other tribes, and cause illness and death by digging their claws into the victims.[17]

Three methods of making are recorded for the northern Arunta and Illpirra. The first is carried out by the Iruntarinia, the Alcheringa or ancestral spirits, who from time to time undergo reincarnation. One place in which this is done is a cave 16 kilometers from Alice Springs, of which the natives have superstitious dread. The spirits are supposed to live in this cave in perpetual sunshine, amid streams of running water. The aspirant sleeps at the mouth of the cave, not venturing to enter, else he would be spirited away forever. A spirit comes at daybreak to the mouth of the cave and, finding the man there, throws an invisible lance, which pierces his neck from behind, passes through his tongue, making therein a large hole, and comes out through his mouth. A second lance pierces the head from ear to ear. The victim falls dead and is carried into the depths of the cave. The Iruntarinia removes the man's internal organs and provides a new set, together with a supply of magical stones on which his power will depend. Later on, the man comes to life again but is for a time insane. When he has partly recovered, he is led back by the spirits to his own people. He remains strange for a few days and then appears with a band of powdered charcoal and fat across his nose. He is recognized as a medicine man but does not practice for about twelve months. In the interval he learns the secrets of the craft from other medicine men. These principally consist of the power to hide about his person, and to produce, small quartz pebbles and pieces of stick and to look preternaturally solemn.[18]

In this interesting method—which is associated with the great ancestors and introducers of culture—the chief experience during seclusion is interpreted as a death, during which new insides and quartz stones are substituted for the old internal organs. Restoration to life follows. The hole in the tongue is genuine, being an outward mark of the real medicine man.

The second method is carried out by the spirits of the Oruncha men of the Alcheringa time, who are mischievous in nature. The procedure is the same as in the first method. The Oruncha of Chauritji, who lives near Alice Springs, occasionally seizes a man, takes him into the earth, and makes a medicine man of him.[19]

Other medicine men are the officiants in the third method. They extract small clear crystals from their bodies and press them slowly and strongly three times along the front of the initiate's legs and up to his breastbone, scoring the skin at intervals to make the crystals enter. The postulant then lies down while they jerk their hands, in which there are crystals, toward him. The scoring is repeated, and a crystal is rubbed on his scalp. A hole is made under the nail of the first finger of the right hand, in order to receive a crystal, and, further, the novice is given meat supposed to contain crystals and water in which small ones have been placed. All this is repeated on the second and third days, after which a hole is made in his tongue. He is then rubbed with grease, a sacred representation on the Oruncha is painted on him, and a fillet of fur string and gum leaves is placed around his head. Instruction is given to the effect that he must remain at the men's camp until his wounds are healed and must observe certain food taboos for a prescribed period. After his return to his own camp, the new doctor sleeps for some time with a fire between himself and his wife, so as to make himself visible to the Oruncha and to make it clear to the latter that he is holding aloof from everyone. Otherwise, the magic power would leave him.[20]

Strehlow, for the western Aranda, gives an account of the making that combines the second and third of the preceding methods. An evil being causes a man to be out of his mind and to run around all night without rest and, while he is doing so, "works" magical stones toward him, which penetrate his body, thighs, breast, tongue, head, and fingertips. The evil being then takes the postulant to the entrance of his dwelling in the west, where he knocks him about until he becomes unconscious, "drives" a kangaroo calf-bone into the back of his head, and inserts magic stones into his shoulders, hips, and stomach. At daybreak two evil beings lead him back to his camp, where their mocking laugh is heard. Two old doctors come out to their new colleague and drive the evil beings away to their abode.

These old doctors now take charge. The postulant recognizes no one, not even his nearest relatives, but they put into his ears magic stones, extracted from their own bodies, so that he will regain his hearing (understanding). They build a hut for him, feed him, and instruct him, especially in the food restrictions and rules of the craft. After this, an old doctor pierces the top of the postulant's right forefinger with a pointed magic stick, to enable him to draw the object that is causing the illness out of a patient's body into his own forefinger and so on to his hand. Later, in the presence of the old man, and while they are chanting a "tongue-hole" song, a doctor cuts a hole in the postulant's tongue; this is to enable him to suck with his tongue the magic out of his patient's body. The young fellow has been under a ban of silence all this time, but it is now lifted at a rite in which the dough of a partly baked damper is sprinkled over his head and the heads of the other men present, and the rest of the loaf is given to him.[21]

This account makes clear what is usually only implied, that the mystic experience is followed by definite ritual acts and operations by old doctors, the masters of the craft. They not only instruct the postulant but magically insert objects into him and in this case make holes in the forefinger and in the tongue.[22] An interesting aspect of the procedure is the public nature of the tongue-piercing. The old men are present, apparently, even though they are not all doctors. This is true also of the final bread ceremony.

The methods in the Unmatjera and Kaitish tribes are essentially the same as in the Arunta. The medicine men are generally made by the spirits of the Iruntarinia class. But a celebrated Unmatjera medicine man said he was made by another practitioner in the following way: A very old doctor threw some of his crystalline stones and killed the novice. Some of the stones when through his head from ear to ear. The doctor then cut out all his insides, intestines, lungs, liver, heart, in fact, everything and left him till next morning, when he placed more of these stones in his body, arms, and legs, and covered his face with leaves. After singing over him until his body was swollen up, he put more stones in him. He then patted him on the head, causing him to "jump up alive," and made him drink water and eat meat containing magic stones. When he awoke, he had forgotten who he was and all the past. Indeed, the old doctor told him that he had killed him a long time ago. On this return to the camp, the people could tell by his strange behavior what had happened. Here, as in the Arunta, the retention of power depends upon the observance of certain restrictions. The medicine man must not eat too much fat or drink anything hot or allow a big ant to bite him.[23]

This account fills what seems to be a lacuna in the Arunta account and shows that in Central Australia, even when the method is of the third type (that is, making by other medicine men), the seclusion is interpreted as a death followed by a restoration, and that during the state of "death," the insides are cut out and magical stones inserted.

The Waramunga medicine men are made in two ways. In one, the agents are spirits of the Iruntarinia type. For example, in a case cited, a man was "boned" by two spirits while asleep, and died. They cut him open, took out his insides, provided him with a new set, and put in his body a little snake that endowed him with the "powers." They then left him. In the meantime, his friends, becoming anxious, searched for him, and eventually an old man found his body and returned to the camp to tell the others that he was dead. Preparations were made for the usual tree burial, and some men went to carry in his body. But by the time they reached him, he had come to life again, and they realized that he had been made a medicine man.[24]

But the great majority are made in the second way, namely, by other medicine men, who must be of the Worgaia tribe. There is very great secrecy regarding this method. The graduates wear through the nose a little structure called a *kupitja,* which is both an emblem of the profession and, in part, a source of their powers. The young doctor believes that it was made by some very powerful old snakes in the Alcheringa and is full of magic. More food restrictions are placed on the newly made medicine man in the Waramunga tribe than farther south. Their infringement causes loss of powers, also sickness, and probably death. Further, a young doctor must bring in the forbidden food for the old ones. While being made, the candidates are allowed no food, drink, or rest and become stupefied. Their insides are cut open, and a new set of organs given. A snake, efficacious because it comes from the Worgaia men, is put into their heads, and finally one of the kupitjas is given to each of them. Such medicine men are called *urtuku*, the general term for snakes.[25]

The medicine men of the Binbinga tribe are made by spirits called Mundadji and Munkaninji, the former being the father of the latter. The following is an example: One man was caught by Mundadji, who killed him, cut him open right down the middle, took out all his insides, exchanged them for his own, and also put a number of sacred stones into the man's body. The younger spirit then came and restored him to life, telling him that he was now a medicine man and showing him how to extract bones and other forms of evil magic. After this, he took him up to the sky and brought him down to the earth close to the man's own camp, where he heard the natives mourning for him, thinking he was dead. He gradually recovered from his dazed condition, and they knew he had been made a medicine man.[26]

The Mara rite is much the same as the Binbinga. Something in the nature of a request is first made by the postulant. He collects a considerable quantity of the fat of various animals, and, making a fire toward sunset in some lonely spot, he burns the fat. The smell, ascending to the sky, attracts the attention of two spirits called Minungarra, who live there. They come down, and, knowing what the man wants, they tell him not to be frightened, as they do not intend to kill him altogether. They make him insensible, cut him open, and take out his insides, which they replace with a set of their own. He is brought to life again and told he is a doctor. Instruction in his craft is then given, after which they take him up to the sky and bring him down near to his camp, where he finds that his friends have been mourning for him.[27]

The *munkani* (doctors) in the Anula tribe are quite distinct from those in any other tribes described by Spencer and Gillen. The profession is strictly hereditary in the members of the Falling Star totem, who are especially associated with two unfriendly spirits living in the sky. The doctors may be of either sex. Strictly speaking, they are wizards or sorcerers, for their powers consist of giving "bones" and not of withdrawing evil magic. This sole evil function distinguishes them from the medicine men of most other tribes. In serious cases, the natives have to call in the assistance of a medicine man from some friendly tribe. Otherwise, they have special incantations that are sung both to oust the evil magic and to prevent it from entering them. The medicine men of the Anula tribe sing to a friendly Alcheringa spirit to make the sick man well. They can see this spirit and also the two unfriendly spirits who live in the sky.[28]

Far Northwestern Queensland

Medicine men of the Pita-Pita tribe (Boulia) are made in several ways. In the usual one, the postulant leaves the camp for three or four days, fasts, and becomes more or less "cranky." While in this state, he sees a nature spirit called Malkari, who makes him a medicine man by inserting in his inside certain small pebbles, bones, quartz crystals, and magical substances. Malkari is a supernatural power who makes everything that the Boulia Aboriginals cannot otherwise account for.[29]

Both here and in the Maitakudi (Cloncurry), the medicine man is termed "the bone-possessor" because he uses a special and very powerful pointer, called *mangani*. It consists of a human or emu bone, connected by human hair or opossum twine with a receptacle that is preferably made from a human shin or arm bone. The victim's life-blood is magically drawn into this receptacle. Medicine men alone can use this "pointer," the potency of which lies in the quartz crystal that passes from it into the body of the victim. The Ulupulu (Ooloopooloo) doctor causes a crane or pelican to go to the victim and point the receptacle, bringing it back with the required blood. This is said to be more potent than the ordinary method. Both systems were taught by Malkari to the Ulupulu, who kept the secret of this latter method, while the other was diffused all over the district.

Karnmari, a water snake, is the officiant in another method of making a medicine man in the Pita-Pita and other tribes in the Boulia district. A death charm, a *mangani*, is pointed by the snake at the postulant. Four or five days later, the medicine men remove from the latter's insides the identical pebble, bone, crystal, or whatever it might be that was put in by the snake. He then recovers and becomes a medicine man. The same magical object may be "inserted" in another novice, even when quite a child, to make him a medicine man. The spirit of a deceased person can also make a medicine man.[30]

Medicine men of the Maitakudi tribe are taught their profession by Tangalagulan, a "nature spirit" or supernatural being. But if the spirit will not make himself patent, the individual has to make a long journey to the Diamantina River, to a certain encampment of the Goa tribe. After having made a present to his teacher, he is put to death and thrown into a waterhole for four days. On the fifth day, he is taken out. A number of fires are lighted around him, and thus his body is smoked quite dry, with the object of getting the water out of him and so making him "all-right and alive again." Instruction is then given about the use of the death charm.[31]

This information for far northwestern Queensland and the Northern Territory Anula tribe refers mainly to the making and powers of sorcerers and the use of the mangani pointer. But the Queensland practitioners can also cure by extracting the material cause of the illness and attributing that object to its sorcerer-owner. The latter, however, is said to have been employed by someone else, and the doctors consult as to the person to be held responsible. Among the Anula, the munkani are only sorcerers. In east Arnhem Land, too, as we shall see, there is a class of magicians whose operations are wholly evil, though there is another class whose work is positive and well disposed.[32]

Arnhem Land

Among the northern clans of the Murngin and Yaernungo tribes there is a belief in magic, but there are no magicians. In the southern and more western clans and tribes, however, magicians, good and evil (sorcerers), are prevalent.

The future sorcerer is taught by his father, father's brother, or mother's brother, the tendency being to get the power almost as a right from one's sorcerer-father. In any case, the novice must associate with the older sorcerer for a killing or two before his power is recognized in his group. The sorcerer's aim is to extract his victim's soul. To do this he may pull the person out of the camp by means of a rope placed around his neck, and then, opening the body beneath the heart, he pierces it with a stick, and catches the blood in a basket. The stopping of the heartbeats is a sign that the soul has been let out. The wound is so healed that no mark is left on the skin. The victim is made conscious, but as he returns to the camp the sorcerer hits him with a club and cuts his body in two several times, the parts flying like leaves and then coming together again. In spite of all this, the victim feels very fit on the day after his "experience," but he becomes sick on the second day and dies on the third.

In an alternative method, the sorcerer may bite a sleeping

man's nasal bone, causing him to open his mouth and take a deep breath, which opens the heart. The soul comes out and goes down the sorcerer's mouth.

In stealing a woman's soul, a large blue fly is sometimes put in her. It flies out of her mouth with her soul. But a woman's soul may also be extracted by an operation on her heart.

The stolen soul seems usually to become a familiar to the sorcerer or else hangs around him and may be detected by a medicine man.[33]

Murngin medicine men are called *marrngit* and have powers of healing, divining a murderer (or soul-stealer), knowing what occurs at a distance, reading another person's thoughts, and exerting control over Muit, the totem python, who makes rain. The profession does not seem to be hereditary. Accounts of two makings have been recorded independently by W. L. Warner and the Reverend T. T. Webb (missionary in the district). In one case, a man, who had been confined to a camp for a week with a sore hip, had a vision. Two familiars (a boy and a girl) spoke to him, with the result that he followed them out and back to camp. At night they sat on his head and shoulders and also flew with the aid of their white feathers to the tops of the trees. Next day, he found them in the bush and, catching them in the hook of his spear-thrower, put them under his arms. But they left him before he returned to camp, telling him they were two *nari*, familiars, and that he must not start to practice his profession yet.

Apparently, the process of getting these spirit-helpers takes some time, for Warner's informant said that during the process he went around very quietly in one place, saying nothing and eating only vegetable food. He made an old doctor his friend, whom he provided with food and tobacco in return for training. Indeed, one of the spirits left the old doctor and came to him. At length, another marrngit, after watching him carefully, said: "He is a true doctor all right; he has some things sitting on his shoulder"; and when one night the rest of the group heard a clicking sound—a kind of beating against the new marrngit's shoulders—all doubts were set at rest.[34]

This making includes

1. a vision of the familiars in the guise of spirit-children, who are henceforth to be the doctor's assistants; and
2. a period of instruction in which both these familiars and an old doctor play roles.

It is, in part, one of seclusion, quietness, and psychic practice in learning to see things inside the sick, around the dead, and at a distance; the training would seem also to include ventriloquism and other devices. No bodily operation is experienced.[35]

Both Webb and Warner describe the making of another doctor, Munyiryir (Moinyerenyer). The latter thinks that two spirit-marrngit (one a male and the other a female) were attracted by some bandicoot that he caught.[36] At any rate, just as he was waking from an after-dinner sleep, one of the spirits half-stunned him, and the other jumped on his chest. He attempted unsuccessfully to call his relations, but the spirit-doctors "thrust all manner of pointed objects into his body." After this, with the help of two younger spirit-doctors, they threw him into a waterhole, and when he began to drown, they pulled him out. The two elder ones then extracted all the pointed objects, so that he felt well again, and told him that he would be able to extract such things from sick people. According to Warner's account, the spirit-doctors opened Munyiryir's eyes, nose, and mouth and blew in his mouth, making him well, after which he hit them on the nose and then, blowing on them, made them well again. They conducted him into a cave occupied by ghosts, marrngit, and python (his chief totem) and then brought him back to camp. The people there, noting his strange behavior and hearing the spirit-marrngit on his shoulders, realized that he was now a doctor.[37]

This trance or vision experience differs from the preceding one, mainly in that it includes a ritual death (or near-death) that apparently enables the doctor to understand the experiences of the victims of sorcery, whom he will later be called upon to cure. It also includes a visit to a cave of ghosts and totemic and other spirits, which no doubt initiates the new doctor into his future association with such beings. It may be that the first informant, Wilijangal, had forgotten, or was not prepared, to divulge this ritual experience of being killed and cured; or it may be that it was possible to become a doctor through a less unpleasant trance experience than Munyiryir's.

In either case, the doctor becomes equipped with spirit marrngit, the means of his knowledge and power. Webb says that these familiars are the spirits of persons long since dead and forgotten. When healing a person by sucking, these familiars go inside the patient and bring the bone out. They also fly to obtain information of what occurs at a distance.[38]

According to a private communication from W. E. Harney, among the Rembarunga, at the head of the Wilton River, if a man sleeps or camps upon the grave of a medicine man, the spirit of the latter shows or gives to him the magic he formerly possessed and used.

The making of medicine men in the Kakadu tribe[39] is associated with the first medicine man, Joemin, and also with a great snake, Numereji, and his descendants. Numereji, at the end of his wanderings, in the long-past, went into the ground at Mungeruauera, where he can still be seen by medicine men. Another sacred spot or camp was made by Joemin at

Mulipaji, where he left some of the blood of a little Numereji snake. He drank some of the blood and carried the rest in a shell. He gave the little snake to his brother, whose eyes he rubbed, so that he might be able to look at the snake. In making his son a medicine man, Joemin caused him to wash himself clean, showed him some of the snake's blood, rubbed it on him, and made him drink some. He then gave him the snake, after which the novice returned to camp and stayed in a new hut for four days with the snake. No woman could come near the hut, which was sacred. When he came into the common camp, he was a medicine man. An important effect of the making was to have keen-sighted eyes, which could look through trees, men, and rocks, and see any distance.

The following was the method used by Joemin in obtaining a snake. He went to a tree in which a child was buried and took out some of its fat, especially the kidney-fat, and both heels. He put the former in the shell. Coming to a big hill, he made a fire at the foot of an anthill and put some of the fat on it. A Numereji came out, which he took, rubbed, and cleaned.[40]

Numereji is associated with the rainbow. The latter is supposed to be Iwaiyu, the shadow-spirit of a Numereji snake, which on spitting makes rain and says: "Up above Iwaiyu, so spittle, my Iwaiyu." It does so in the form of a rainbow, which is supposed to stop the rain. On melting away, the rainbow is supposed to go back underground to Numereji. Numereji can also cause a child to be born dead by taking away its spirit or Iwaiyu while the mother is bathing.[41]

The medicine man's association with Numereji is of special value in a region where one's spirit part can be lured away or stolen. Thus, if a woman drinks water or eats fish out of a deep waterhole while her child is still young, the child's *iwaiyu* spirit will run into the waterhole and be drawn down and eaten by a Numereji snake. But the medicine man knows how to attract the spirit up again, and seeing and grasping it, he puts it in the mother's head, and it passes through her breast into the child again when the child drinks.

Likewise, if a mischievous spirit from another tribe steals a young man's soul, a medicine man, with a Numereji snake under his arm, can frighten the mischievous spirit and rescue and replace the soul in the boy.[42]

The Kakadu medicine men are thus connected with what corresponds to the dreamtime and its culture-givers through the first medicine men and Numereji, the rainbow snake.

Among the Daly River tribes there is a belief in the existence of *mamakpik*, or sorcerers, who are said to take a person's kidney-fat, and also of socially useful doctors, *miumdakar*. W. E. H. Stanner reports that a man becomes a doctor by associating in dreams with the spirits of the dead and loses his power once he ceases to dream of them.[43]

Referring to one of these tribes, the Mulukmuluk, W. E. Harney tells me that a man who becomes a doctor is attacked in some secluded spot by numerous devils. These kill him by splitting him open along the abdomen, and they then cook and eat him. The devils carefully collect the bones into a basket, which two of them rock until the man becomes alive again. He is then asked what type of *kurang*, or doctor, he desires to be, specializing in extracting deadly poison (*mauia*) or in extracting bits of bone, stones, and suchlike. After this experience, he can learn the art of healing.

Among the Wardaman, the medicine man receives power from Wolgara, the spirit who judges and guards the dead. Wolgara meets the aspirant in the dense scrub and there fights him. But in a dream, he is brought back to life by the ministration of the black hawk, who heals the wound without leaving a mark. Wolgara then summons a white hawk, which breathes life into the postulant, with the result that he returns to camp, but now endowed with healing power.[44]

In both the Mulukmuluk and the Wardaman makings, a spirit or spirits officiate; the trance experience is one of death (caused by a fight and being cut about or open), followed by restoration to life, and endowment with new power, that of a medicine man. Specialist training must follow.

The Kimberley Division, Northwest Australia

In the Djerag and Djaru tribes, East Kimberley, the medicine man is made by Kulabel, the rainbow serpent, who kills the aspirant when he is bathing at some waterhole. He feels that something has gone through, or happened to, his ears. He becomes sick and mad and then receives his power. As in other regions, especially in Central Australia, the medicine man loses his power if he has a hot drink.[45]

Dr. Phyllis Kaberry includes the Djerag and Djaru along with other tribes of East Kimberley, such as the Lunga, Malngin, and Miriwun, in her references to medicine men and medicine women. The medicine man (*baramambin*) can cure illness, visit the spirits of the dead to obtain magical, curative, and even injurious powers, and "divine" a murderer (that is, conduct an inquest). The medicine woman (*baramambil*) possesses the first two powers but not the third; this means that dealing with a sorcerer (generally attributed to another tribe) and possibly causing his death is considered a man's work.

Medicine men and women are associated with the rainbow serpent, Kalera, in their making, but it seems that only the male doctors can approach this being with impunity, although Dr. Kaberry states that, like the former, the baramambil may obtain magical stones from Kalera. The dead are visited by going up to the sky on a string.

In the making, the postulant is taken away in her sleep by the spirits of the dead, given instruction, and returned to the camp, where for a few days she may be a "little bit mad, him deaf, can't hear." Later she bathes in a pool where Kalera is known to dwell and receives from him oval pieces of pearl-shell (*pindjauwindja*) and magical stones, or these may be inserted in her side. If her mother were a doctor, she might receive instruction from her.[46]

In the Forrest River district, Northern Kimberley, a medicine man, *malimber gude*, receives his powers ultimately from the rainbow snake, Brimurer or Ungur. He is made by a fully qualified practitioner. The method is said by several informants to be somewhat as follows: The postulant is taken up to the sky by the medicine man in one of two ways. A string hangs down from the sky, with crosspieces on which the two men sit. The string, in moving up, also moves sideways, from the south to the north, for example. This picture may be based on the rainbow. The alternative way is for the older man to take the form of a skeleton, sit astride the rainbow snake and pull himself up with an arm-over-arm action on a rope. The postulant has been made quite small, like an infant in arms, and put in a pouch, which the medicine man fastens on himself. When near the top, the latter throws the postulant out of the pouch onto the sky, thus making him "dead." Having reached the sky, the doctor inserts into the young man some little rainbow snakes and some quartz crystals, *maban*: I do not know if the medicine man is supposed to obtain these magical articles up in the sky or takes them up with him, for he can get them down below at the foot of the rainbow. He goes along to a waterhole and, seeing the rainbow snake there, catches hold of it, obtains these magical objects, and also another type, called *kandela*, resembling crooked teeth. These, when inserted into the postulant, make him clever.

After the older man has brought the other back to the earth in the same manner as he took him up, he inserts more of these magical objects in him through the navel, after which he wakes him up with a magic stone. The young man returns to his normal size, if he had been changed, and next day he himself tries to go up to the sky. He receives instruction in his profession. This includes the use of quartz crystals and oval, elongated pieces of pearl-shell, *pindjauandja,* which he carries about with him—not in his "inside." He learns how to project these into a victim through his back, thus causing his sickness and death, and also how to withdraw evil magic. He learns, too, the more homely remedies for ills, such as tying string around or rubbing the affected part.

He is trained as a medium, for a medicine man can see the spirits of the dead, whether they be about the bush or hanging around the grave, and can detect the spirit of a living murderer hanging around the grave of his victim. He also learns the technique of conducting an inquest and of playing his part in revenge. I have no record of any privations that the postulant has to undergo, but it is hardly likely that there would be none.

The medicine men apparently take care not to let the ordinary people learn the secret of their powers or the "make-believe" on which it is at least partly founded. Thus, when a doctor sees a rainbow passing across a big waterhole, he warns all the people not to go in there, or else they will be drowned. The rainbow is said to be the action of the water snake in stopping the rain.

The reduction of the postulant to the size of an infant and carrying him in a pouch, which is likened to a kangaroo's pouch, suggests that the rite is pictured as one of rebirth. This is an extra detail to the usual method, which is also present in this case; in it the aspirant is killed, provided with new insides, taken up to the sky, and finally wakened up or brought to life again.

These beliefs about the making and powers of medicine men are common to all the Forrest River tribes and also to the Wolyamidi. I did not hear that the medicine men of these tribes practiced fat-taking. A Wolyamidi informant stated that he had heard of it on the eastern side of Cambridge Gulf. Of course, this may have been merely a case of accusing the other party, feeling that the practice was condemned by whites. A Forrest River medicine man, however, does spear a victim. But when he does so, a sky-being, Tjadingin, who resembles an emu, comes down and closes the wound, so that no mark remains.[47]

The Ungarinyin medicine man is called *bainman*. This term is used in Dampier Land to denote certain objects inside the medicine man with which his special powers are associated. The Ungarinyin medicine man "finds" Wonjad, the rainbow serpent, in the water. The latter is also called Ungud, the equivalent of Ungur, one of the Forrest River names for the rainbow serpent. The use of the same term, which denotes the heroic dreamtime and the cult-heroes, is not surprising, for the eastern hordes of the Ungarinyin come into contact with some of the Forrest River district tribes. It is probable that the making and powers of medicine men in the districts are similar.[48]

According to an Ungarinyin informant, the medicine men draw prestige from the eclipses of the moon and sun. One of them, probably an unfriendly one, causes the face of the heavenly body to be covered with blood. The people are then frightened. After a while, another medicine man goes up to the sky in a dream. When he returns, he tells his countrymen that he has made the sun (or moon) better. A medicine man also goes up to the sky after a lot of rain, hits Jandad, the thunder-being, with a stone, and thus stops the rain.

In the Nyul-Nyul, Djaber-djaber, Bard, and Djaui tribes, the powers of a medicine man, *djalngokora* (*djangagor* in Bard), are associated with various objects called *bainman* inside the body of the practitioner. These are *binji-binj*, narrow pieces of pearl-shell about 15 centimeters long and pointed at one end, thought to have been in him since his birth, although they are the same as the binji-binj ornaments worn by men in their headbands at corroborees; shiny white glassy stones (quartz crystals); small bull-roarer–shaped sticks about 15 or 20 centimeters long, called *koranad*, kept in the small of their backs; and a small snake or perhaps a small dog or a small kangaroo, or some such. Such a spirit reptile or animal is termed *djalng*, a word denoting both totem and magical power. It warns its possessor of danger and will also go out to do services for him, such as gaining information of events at a distance. This djalng, or totemic assistant, is included in another term, *rai* (invisible). For example, I was told that a certain lad would be a medicine man because he had three rai, namely, turkey, fish, and his spirit-double. Only medicine men could see rai.[49]

Some medicine men claim to be able to make storms, hot weather, and so on and to be able to travel around in the air and see everything; this latter power is called *mamaror*. They say that they can also drop sickness from the air, but I could find no instance of this, nor of any black magic. But they are credited with *mirua*, or the power of taking the caul-fat, especially from boys, without leaving a mark. The medicine man has a little bag in which he carries stones, hair, shell, and other objects.

In treating a sick person, the medicine man rubs the afflicted part, generally the abdomen, and takes something away. This may be a material object or not. The rubbing is usually severe and causes vomiting. He also appears to take something from his own body with his hand and press it into the body of the patient.[50]

A person may be born with magical "insides." He has a strange look in his eyes and is recognized by the medicine men as one of them. When he coughs, he might drop a little shell.

A person may be made. The aspirant asks a qualified man to initiate him. This person puts him to sleep and cuts open his abdomen and cleans it out with his magical shell and other instruments. He might replace the aspirant's insides with a new set, or he might leave the old ones, but in either case, he inserts magical objects. He then closes the incision, puts white feathers on it, and runs a fire-stick, *madagor*, along it to heat it. No mark remains. After this, he brings him to life again. The new medicine man is sick for a little while. He receives training in his profession and must get permission from older medicine men before practicing.

One old informant said that the aspirant was not cut open, but that the operator put a small snake and also shell into him while he was asleep.

From Bard and Djaui informants, I learned that the medicine man takes a magical object, such as a stone, shell, or snake, from his insides and puts it inside the sick person; it gathers the badness and comes out of itself. The medicine man, who alone sees it, picks it up, washes it, and puts it back in himself. Some medicine men have "little children" in their insides who can be used in the same way.

It was admitted by the Bard that a medicine man could cause sickness, but not unto death, by touching a person in a dream with *kalakor*, an initiation bull-roarer; this might be done at the request of an injured person, for example, one whose wife had been stolen.

The Karadjeri doctor (*djangangora*) is made by Bulang, a water snake, which can be seen in the sky. His powers depend on the possession of magical substances, called *maban*, the term used for them at both Forrest River in the north and Laverton a long way to the southeast.[51]

Notes

1. E. J. Eyre, *Journals of Expeditions of Discovery into Central Australia* (London: T. & W. Boone, 1845), vol. 2, p. 359. Meyer, "The Encounter Bay Tribe," in Woods, *Native Tribes*, p. 197, says that the natives of Encounter Bay apply the term *melapar* (sorcerer) to the Adelaide and more northern tribes, believing that "they have the power of transforming themselves into birds, trees, etc."

2. Howitt, *Native Tribes*, p. 405. J. M. Sutton, "The Adjahdurah Tribe of Aborigines on Yorke's Peninsula," *South Australian Geographical Journal* 2 (1887–88): 19, says that the sorcerer would lie beside the corpse and have communion with the soul. This writer calls the Narrang-ga the Adjadura, Howitt, *Native Tribes*, p. 67. W. J. Kuhn in L. Fison and A. W. Howitt, *Kamilaroi and Kurnai* (Melbourne: G. Robertson, 1880), p. 287, refers to the hereditary nature of the profession. Kuhn says that the men called Gureldes professed to learn corroborees, songs, and dances from departed spirits. He refers to this tribe (or part of it) as the Turra.
3. C. Wilhelmi, "Manners and Customs of the Australian Natives, in Particular of the Port Lincoln District," *Royal Society of Victoria* 5 (1862): 182–83.
4. Howitt, *Native Tribes*, p. 313.
5. Elkin, Field Notes.
6. R. M. and C. H. Berndt, "A Preliminary Report," *Oceania* 14, no. 1:56–61. The information obtained by R. M. Berndt regarding the making of doctors is especially reliable, both because of his knowledge of his native informants and because he went into the field with an adequate understanding of the problems involved. For the cultural grouping of these tribes, see Elkin, "The Social Organization of South Australian Tribes," pp. 60–62.
7. I was informed that *kalaia* made the "law" in this region.
8. Elkin, Field Notes.
9. Ibid. Also A. P. Elkin, "Burial Practices in North-Eastern and Western South Australia," *Oceania* 7, no. 3:291.
10. Elkin, Field Notes. Also above, pp. 30–32, and below, pp. 110, 116, 120.
11. Berndt and Vogelsang, "The Initiation of Native Doctors in the Dieri Tribe, South Australia," *Records of South Australian Museum* 6: 376–77.
12. Howitt, *Native Tribes*, pp. 358–60. Bone-pointing is widely practiced in this tribe, and the human ingredient that forms part of the instrument generally used does not limit its use to medicine men. This practice started in the days of the Mura-Mura heroes. S. Gason, "The Dieyerie Tribe," in Woods, *Native Tribes*, pp. 275–76. M. E. B. Howitt, "Some Native Legends from Central Australia," *Folklore* 13 (1902): 405–6.
13. Berndt and Vogelsang, "Initiation of Native Doctors," p. 374. Elkin, "Burial Practices," pp. 281–82. There is no record of fat-taking by Dieri medicine men or other persons, but there is a suggestion that one's kidney-fat may be taken by spirits. Thus, if a man kills or hunts a crow, the *mungara* (spirit of the crow) will cut out his kidney-fat. It is also dangerous to collect wood in the evening, because the *kutji* could cut open one's abdomen and extract the kidney-fat. O. Siebert, "Sagen und Sitten der Dieri und Nachbarstamme in Zentral-Australien," *Globus* 92 (1910): 56.
14. Berndt and Vogelsang, "Initiation of Native Doctors," pp. 375–76.
15. Siebert, "Sagen und Sitten," p. 55.

16. Elkin, Field Notes.
17. Spencer and Gillen, *Native Tribes*, pp. 530–33. Location of the Mungaberra is unknown.
18. Ibid., pp. 523–25. The details of the bodily experience here are similar to what I recorded concerning one magical cause of death in the Great Victorian Desert, far to the southwest. The victim is "choked" by pushing a "stick" (invisible, of course) through his collarbone, neck, and tongue, and inserting little stones and arm blood in his ears, which are pulled, to make him deaf. In the Unmatjera and Kaitish rites, magical stones were thrown so as to go through the postulant's head from ear to ear.
19. Ibid., p. 526. There are occasionally women doctors in these tribes. They are usually made by the Oruncha but sometimes also by the Iruntarinia. In either case the method is the same as that for men.
20. Ibid., p. 526–29.
21. C. Strehlow, *Die Aranda*, vol. 4, pp. 38–41. On page 42, a similar but shorter account is given of the making in the Loritja tribe.
22. Spencer and Gillen, *Native Tribes*, p. 523, said it was impossible to say how this hole was made in the tongue in the case in which the doctor was made by spirits, but thought it must have been made by the postulant himself.
23. Spencer and Gillen, *Northern Tribes*, pp. 480–81.
24. Ibid., pp. 481, 484.
25. Ibid., pp. 484–86. W. E. Harney understands that in the Waramunga and Tjingili tribes, a doctor can impart his magic to another man by letting him swallow the "magic snake" of healing—a form of worm without teeth and with a jointed head and tail. The snake is then removed from his side. (W. E. Harney is author of *Taboo*, short stories dealing with culture contact in the Northern Territory, where he spent nearly thirty years and acquired much valuable knowledge of Aboriginal life and belief.)
26. Spencer and Gillen, *Northern Tribes*, pp. 487–88. When a medicine man operates, the younger spirit is supposed to be watching nearby. The bone, when extracted, is thrown, unseen by those around, in the direction where the spirit is sitting. The latter, on the request of the doctor, grants permission for the bone to be shown to the natives.
27. Ibid., p. 488. Among the powers of the Mara medicine men is that of climbing at night by means of a rope invisible to ordinary mortals, up to the sky, where he can hold converse with the star people. Binbinga medicine men, like those of the Mara, can see the two unfriendly sky-spirits as well as the friendly spirit who lives in the woods. Ibid., p. 501.
28. Ibid., pp. 488–89, 502. The term for doctor (sorcerer), *munkani*, is probably the western Queensland word *mangani* (a death charm). See Roth, *Superstition, Magic*, p. 29. The Mara term for doctor is *mungurni*. Spencer and Gillen, *Northern Tribes*, p. 488.

29. Roth, *Superstition, Magic,* p. 29. Roth, *Ethnological Studies,* p. 253.
30. Roth, *Superstition, Magic,* p. 29. Roth, *Ethnological Studies,* p. 153.
31. Roth, *Superstition, Magic,* p. 30. Roth, *Ethnological Studies,* p. 153. Neither the Maitakudi nor the Goa practiced circumcisions, but as they adjoined and mixed with circumcision tribes, with whom, as among themselves, sorcery of the mangani type played a very important part, I have included them here. Possibly the Maikulan, north-central Queensland, also an uncircumcised tribe, almost adjoining the Maitakudi on the east, could be included here, as some of its beliefs seem to be the same: the doctors have association with *lim-been-jargolong,* spirits of the dead in trees, E. Palmer, "Notes on Some Australian Tribes," p. 291; while the Maitakudi doctors can be initiated by the spirit of the dead person, *lim-bi-ja-koo-lun,* Roth, *Ethnological Studies,* p. 153. But no reference to mangani magic has been recorded for the Maikulan.
32. W. E. Harney, however, tells me that the Anula have medicine women who have received power and can heal the sick. Of course, this may be a development since Spencer and Gillen worked in the region.
33. Warner, *Black Civilization,* pp. 193–98. Webb, "The Making of a Marrngit," p. 336, says the sorcerers are called *ragalk.*
34. Warner, *Black Civilization,* pp. 212–14.
35. Webb summarizes what seems to be information obtained from the same medicine man but at another time. The man concerned (Wilijangal, called Wilidjungo by Warner) had a presentiment, while returning from gathering honey, that the marrngit spirits were approaching him. His bag got lighter, and during the night they entered it and made their sharp clicking sound. After this he became ill and unconscious, and then events went on as described above, except that there is no mention of the old doctor, and that there is the additional claim by Wilijangal that he later acquired another pair of familiar spirits. These two keep him informed about sorcerers, and the other two give him power to heal. Webb, "The Making of a Marrngit," pp. 337–39.
36. W. E. Harney tells me that in east Arnhem Land an aspirant kills a bandicoot and hangs it up for four days. He crushes it with a stone and anoints his body with this substance. He now sleeps by himself, and the spirit of healing comes to him in the form of a bird and gives to him power to remove objects from sick people. This suggests that the smell of the bandicoot in a rotting condition (as Webb's account also suggests) is a necessary part of the rite and prelude to the vision.
37. Webb, "The Making of a Marrngit," pp. 339–41. Warner, *Black Civilization,* pp. 215–16. This introduction to the python, who controls rain, enables the medicine man hereafter, in case of a dangerous flood, with the help of his familiars, to dive into the water, catch Muit, the totemic python, and send him down the totemic well again. The flood then goes down. Ibid., pp. 218–19.

38. W. E. Harney writes that in east Arnhem Land a spirit disguised as a bird, e.g., a kingfisher, will fly around a man's head and give him power to predict future events. Obviously, this bird is a marrngit.
39. This is one of the tribes in the northwest corner of Arnhem Land that had not adopted circumcision before the spread of that rite was stopped by contact with white settlement and by consequent disintegration. I have, however, left it in its geographical context with the Murngin and Rembarunga tribes, with which it had much ceremonial life in common, e.g., the *Djangoan* rite and *maraian* objects. See Spencer and Gillen, *Native Tribes*, and Warner, *Black Civilization*. Moreover, the Murngin and other tribes of northeast Arnhem Land, like the Daly River tribes, while practicing circumcision, do not practice subincision, an indication, in my opinion, that the introduction and adoption of the former rite into the region is comparatively recent.
40. Spencer and Gillen, *Native Tribes*, pp. 290–99. Medicine man is *marunga* or *maringa* or *mari*.
41. Ibid., p. 326. There is a similar association of the snake and the rainbow in the Anula tribe. In the far-past times, a dollar-bird had as a mate a snake called Ngurulia, who lived in a particular waterhole named Upintjara, "and when he wanted rain to fall, he used to spit up into the sky, with the result that the rainbow appeared and was shortly after followed by clouds and then by rain." A man of the dollar-bird totem can now make rain at this waterhole by singing over a snake and an imitation rainbow. Certain taboos are observed regarding this spot. Spencer and Gillen, *Northern Tribes*, pp. 314–15.

    The Waramunga, too, believe that the rainbow issues from the vent of a water snake called Nappakandattha, in the form of a red oval plate. The great mystic snake called Wollunqua can also place it in the sky at pleasure, but they have no idea that it either prevents or assists the fall of rain. Ibid., p. 631.
42. Ibid., pp. 346, 434.
43. W. E. H. Stanner, "The Daly River Tribes," *Oceania* 4, no. 1:25. Knut Dahl, *In Savage Australia*, p. 21, says the devil (*barrang, bolongo*, and *wurrang*) may take up its residence in a man and give him power to kill his foes by magic. At night he may go through the air until he stoops over his victim and takes his fat.
44. Harney, personal communication.
45. Elkin, Field Notes.
46. Kaberry, *Aboriginal Woman*, pp. 170, 185, 211–12, 217, 251–52.
47. Elkin, Field Notes. The Forrest tribes include the Yeidji, Andedja, and others. See A. P. Elkin, *Studies in Australian Totemism*, Oceania Monograph no. 2, pp. 79–80.
48. Elkin, Field Notes. A. Capell, "Mythology in Northern Kimberley, North-West Australia," *Oceania* 9, no. 4:394, says the "sorcerer is possessed of

Ungud, who comes to him as he sleeps by a sacred pool and this Ungud may desert him later, when he ceases to be a sorcerer."

49. Elkin, *Studies in Australian Totemism*, pp. 52–58.
50. Father Ernest Worms tells me in a letter July 27, 1944, that he saw a Nyul-Nyul medicine man operate in the following way on his own son, who was unconscious as a result of falling from a horse. The father knelt down by the boy, took his own djalng, with an appropriate gesture, out of his chest and pressed and rubbed it into the body of his son, who soon came to. Father Worms adds that the doctor's equipment includes a white jelly fish, which is used for rubbing into his body.

    In his "Aboriginal Place Names in Kimberley, Western Australia," *Oceania* 14, no. 4:299, Father Worms says that the victim of Rai-Dog magic could be saved by a medicine man who was able to dream of the hiding place of the abducted soul by winding the hair brow-band around his head. He slept beside his patient, after which he would visit the Dog Stone (a rai place), pull the soul out of the hollow (in it), put it in his chest, and rub it into the body of his friend, who would then quickly recover.
51. Elkin, Field Notes. In the Bard tribe it is only a *djangagor* who can bring a kalakor out of the sacred ground, for he knows everything. See also *Studies in Australian Totemism*, pp. 53–57.

PART III

Aboriginal Men of High Degree in a Changing World

CHAPTER 5

Mystic Experience: Essential Qualification for Men of High Degree

The future of the "Order" of men of high degree depends on an unbroken succession of qualified persons. Only by and through them can the knowledge, psychic insight, mystic experience, and personality authority that distinguish the Order be passed on. The selection, testing, reception, and instruction of new members are their responsibility, and they themselves must keep certain rules of life and observe taboos, or else they lose their power, status, and influence. In this survey I have reached the threshold of the corpus of belief and ritual that distinguishes the Order, but little further. In the course of one or two periods of fieldwork with a "tribe," at least until recently, an anthropologist might have become aware of a few men of high degree, perhaps only one, or perhaps not one. Moreover, such men were usually reserved, and also spoke little English, while the anthropologist did not have command of the native language. Hence, they could not discuss adequately the philosophical and psychological aspects of that triune system of specialist knowledge, faith, and ritual that was the basis of their craft.

Since the publication of the first edition of this book, further information has become available, especially on the mystic experience involved in being "made" a medicine man. When referring in 1971 to the death not long before of a person whom he considered to be the last of the Western Aranda medicine men, Professor T. G. H. Strehlow said that as a young man the deceased had had a strange visionary experience after which he "sat about in a state of trance for some time." "He was then deemed a fit candidate for admission to the order of medicine men and was put through the whole ritual in spite of once running away in terror from the grimness of his ordeal."[1] He was a man of high degree.

The High Degree: Northern New South Wales

I have mentioned in chapter 3 the fear that caused some postulants in the Wailwan (Weilwan) tribe, to whom I spoke in 1944, to flee from the ritual of making. Thirty years later I came across an unpublished manuscript prepared by R. H. Mathews early this century on medicine men among the Wailwan and other tribes of northwestern New South Wales.[2] It shows that the experience of being made a medicine man in a particular region varied little from generation to generation. In this epitomized account

1. The postulant, tired out by a long day's hunting, was settled down at night by a grave; small fires were lit around him, on which green leaves smeared with goanna fat were thrown; this added to the awesomeness of his situation because burning fat on any ordinary occasion, especially at night, was forbidden.
2. An old man warned him that spirits, whom he "heard"

nearby, would put a white stone into his body through the back of his neck or the top of his shoulder.

3. Next morning the young fellow reported to the "old" doctors what he was expected to see and believed he saw in his fear or dreams during the night.
4. He was then taken to an isolated place to sleep; it was haunted by spirits who, he was told, would take out his kidney-fat or perhaps the whole of his insides and give him a fresh lot.
5. After this, he received instruction in tribal mythology and ritual and was allowed to assist in the ritual and manipulative actions required in the practice of his profession.

In the meantime, the men of high degree had conferred on him a personal totem, his *yerradha,* which would assist him in his work, warn him of danger, and protect him.

We see in this the authority of the clever men, and their use of isolation, suggestion, and fear, and the postulant's conditioning and readiness for what he should see and experience. Thus his "conversion" or transformation was effected.

In the late 1940s, during fieldwork in northeastern New South Wales and southeastern Queensland, I recorded information that widened our knowledge of medicine men and their making. Thus, C. S., a Bigumbal tribesman from Goondiwindi, had been made at Barambah, both places being in southeastern Queensland. The former was in the northeastern group of what may be termed the Kamilaroi ritual community, in which the Weilwan were in its southwestern group. Barambah was a government settlement for Aborigines from southern Queensland. The tribes in the Barambah district were closely associated in ritual with the Bandjelang of the north coast and hinterland of new South Wales.

C. S. was taken by a friend, a clever man, to a burial place to sleep all night. A fire on which fat was burned was so placed that the smoke blew across the grave. His guide and guardian watched to ensure that the spirits did not kill him, thus introducing the aspect of fear. The spirits did come to C. S. in a dream, took him away, and put "things" in him to give him magical power.

Further details of this ritual procedure as it was practiced in his tribal region were given me by C., of Cabbage Tree Island, Richmond River, a very knowledgeable Bandjelang man. A senior clever man took the postulant to a hilly region for three days and, having announced their presence to the spirits, made a camp for him and also one for himself about 30 meters away. The spirits took the postulant to another place in the mountains while he was asleep and put "things" in him. He remained out there three months and got "all he needed" for his profession. This included magic "ropes" (cords), which "live in certain clever waterholes." My informant had seen them rising up. The would-be doctor-man gets the ropes by drinking water or by putting his hands or feet in it. He becomes clever, that is, endowed with magical power.

Such rope can serve as actual rope, although invisible. Thus, near the close of their initiation into manhood and tribal secret life, the initiates are led to a bare tree on top of a peak. On the trunk and limbs of the tree two doctor-men, supported by their "clever ropes," had engraved designs of animals, weapons, and symbols. There the initiates see one of the doctors "sitting" with folded arms and with his legs around the bare upright trunk. Clever ropes hold him there (but to the onlooker it seems miraculous, my informant said). The newly initiated on a given signal rush to the heap of shavings from the engravings at the foot of the tree and throw them up at the man above. The bull-roarer is swung, and they are shown stones of symbolic significance. They are warned by a clever man not to tell anybody what they have seen. To emphasize his words this clever man produces from his stomach a large and "pretty" white stone that will tell him if they do so, in which event the new men will be put to death by spear or by magic. He then throws this big stone into his own mouth and swallows it. Old men explained that it melts and forms again in his stomach. The initiates then pass through the smoke fire and return to camp life.

A clever man can get an individual assistant-totem, bird or animal, by going to the bird's or animal's "clever place," its sacred, mythological center, its "dreaming" (to use a widespread north and west-central Australian term). This totem can be sent away both to take and to gather information.

Another Bandjelang elder, W. P., from Woodenbong near the Queensland border, said that a postulant for this higher degree goes into the bush and camps near a spring, where he fasts for several weeks. There he feels and hears the "clever things" coming on him during the night. These things are the ropes. For crystals (*nyurum*), however, he goes to the mountains, and while camped there he hears something come up to him, which could be his protector, his individual totem. So he picks it up.

A practicing Bandjelang clever man, A. C., from Tabulam, 65 kikometers south of Woodenbong, whom I met in 1946, confirmed this. In his making he went to the mountains for revelations. He fasted for two or three months. His father took him there but after a while left him by himself. His teacher was Biruganba, the sky cult-hero, while two of Biruganba's sisters (the Koinganbi) showed him everything. He saw a carpet snake coiled up on the water in a cave and went to touch it for medicine (magic power), but the snake took him under the water and then up to the top of the mountain. A. C. had a goanna for his assistant-totem, which he kept inside himself. He also had a rope (*nandiri*) and crystal. His powers included the ability to fly at night to distant places (presumably by means of the rope) and to cure sick persons with his right hand, in which he had "something" (rope).[3]

The High Degree: Northern Kimberley, Western Australia

In 1928 I knew an Aboriginal man, Yaobeda, of the Ungarinyin (Ngarinjin) tribe of Walcott Inlet region in Northern Kimberley. I recorded his genealogy, but I was not aware that he was a medicine man. Ten years later, Dr. Helmut Petri (leader of the Frobenius research team) noted that Yaobeda was the incarnation of the Wandjina Kaluru, the mythical hero associated with rain. He added that the Aborigines were firmly convinced that this old medicine man had always existed and would never die a normal death. Like the heroes of mythical times, he would go into the earth one day and change himself into an Unggud snake. As his genealogy showed that he was born in the usual way, and as he later died, the reference is to his pre-existent spirit form as Kaluru, or Wandjina rain hero, which, after the death of his body, returned to the water as an Unggud (creation-time) snake. But to have recorded a discussion of the meaning of this would have been invaluable.

Dr. Petri and Dr. Lommel, a member of his team, who worked among the neighboring Unambal (Wunambal) tribe, also in 1938, were not able to publish their reports until the decade following World War II, several years after the publication of the first edition of *Aboriginal Men of High Degree*.[4]

During the ten years between 1928, the year of my work among the Ungarinyin, and that of Dr. Petri in 1938, the Aborigines had improved their English, a result mainly of working on Munja Aboriginal Cattle Station, Walcott Inlet. Consequently, at least some of them became better informants, and so Dr. Petri obtained more material on medicine men and their making than I did.

During his initiation a young man would get the idea of being a *banman* or *bainman* (doctor-man), and if he had dreams or visions of water, pandanus, and bark when near a water place, he was said to be chosen by Unggud to be a banman. A vision of his dream-totem's visit to heaven would have the same significance. After his initiation into manhood, he went with a medicine man to the water place where he felt that "Unggud had killed him." He sees the same Unggud rise out of the ground or the water, but in its "very essence," which is visible only to medicine men. He sees the giant "snake" with its arms, hands, and a feather "crown." He faints and is led by Unggud to a cool and dry part of a subterranean cave, where his transformation into a banman takes place. Unggud gives him a new brain, puts in his body white quartz crystals, which give secret strength, and reveals to him his future duties. He may remain unconscious for some time, but when he wakes he has a great feeling of inner light. He is certain of being equal to Unggud. Instruction, guidance, and experience follow for many months, even years.[5]

The newly made doctor learns to see and understand hidden things. He will be able to see before his inner eye past and future events and "happenings in other worlds." He learns to read other people's thoughts and recognize their secret worries, to cure illnesses with the "medicine" stones, to put himself in a trance, and to send his *ya-yari* (his dream familiar) from his body to gather information.

The psychic element in these talents is clearly all-pervasive. It is termed *miriru* and comes from Unggud. Fundamentally it is the capacity bestowed on the medicine man to go into a dream state or trance with its possibilities. Indeed, miriru makes him like a Wandjina, having the same abilities as the heroes of "creation times."[6]

When the new man of high degree feels proficient, he

gives a public performance. He and his teacher go to the water place where he had his inspiration to become "doctor." They both plunge in and come to the surface riding on the Unggud-serpent's back in front of the spectators who have gathered there. These latter, however, do not see the Unggud but only the two medicine men and the great waves stirred up by Unggud's giant body. Unggud then throws quartz crystals on the bank, which are collected by the men present and cherished as symbols of the Unggud. In this way, the new doctor's position, prestige, and power are established, just as in central and western New South Wales the clever fellows preserve their reputation and ability by displays, especially with the magic cord.

Dr. Lommel was convinced that this was a case of mass hypnotism. So too for the Wunambal tribe: Coming to the water place, the group sits with the doctor-man and chants until they go into a trance. He then takes a great snake out of the water, sits on its back, and flies through the air very rapidly; indeed, so fast that even other medicine men see only the quivering tail. After some time it settles in the midst of those present. The doctor-man kills one of them and cuts him up with a stone knife, and all partake, along with the Unggud snake, of the "offering." He cleans the victim's bones and places them down in reverse order to what they should be. The other men sweep the snake back to the place from which it came, while the banman touches and rubs the dead man's bones and sings a magic chant over them until they become clothed again with flesh, and the dead person comes to life. He then draws out of his navel a second Unggud snake, which both the doctor and the restored man mount and fly back to the others. After this all come out of their trance experience, but none of them except the banman remember anything that happened. A few days later the "revived" victim dies.

Obviously, this display was believed to be associated with a magical death. Lommel refers to it as an offering that the medicine man had to make from time to time to Unggud, or else the latter would take away his magical power. To meet this condition, he watches out for an enemy whom he can get rid of in this manner.[7]

A somewhat similar feature, however, has been reported from Kalumburu, an isolated mission in the lower Drysdale–King Edward Rivers area, north of Wunambal tribal territory. Two medicine men and their Unggud snakes struggle in the sky until one pair is crushed and falls down dead. Northern Wunambal and their northern and northeastern neighbors have been in contact with missionary activities in the area for several decades. A psychiatrist, accompanying an anthropological research team in 1963 to Kalumburu, obtained a little information from six elderly medicine men, *punmun* (banman) living there but only after long and mostly fruitless conversations.[8]

As in the Ungarinyin and southern Wunambal clans, the doctor-man is closely associated with the Unggur (Unggud) snake from the time he is selected for the profession. His initiating doctor takes some scum off the pool near Kalumburu settlement. This scum, which is Unggur's spittle, is pill-rolled into a ball and inserted into the boy's navel. The Unggur snake hatches out and grows in his belly, as he knows from the cold feeling there. And though he is trained by a practitioner, his prestige and power come from the Unggur snake.

To publicize this he may call up the latter. He puts one end of a reed or bamboo, which holds a magic stone or other substance, into his navel, and the other end into the Unggur pool. The snake rises up vertically and creeps onto dry land, where he transforms his back into a canoelike shape. All medicine men present may go aboard and paddle into the sky a long way before returning to the pool. This is a variation of the doctors' riding on Unggur's back. Though when doctors of opposing tribes fight with each other because of sorcery charges, they mount their respective Unggur and fight in the sky until one of them and his Unggur drop down dead to the ground. Presumably this is a psychic display of mass hypnotism.

A medicine man's power is mediated through his collection of the strongest available magic (*tjagolo*), which only he possesses because he alone dares to dive into Unggur's pool to look for them. In the Ungarinyin account, as mentioned above, the new graduate and his tutor dive into the Unggur water from which the Unggur (surely by the hands of the banman) throws maban (magic stones) onto the bank.

The High Degree: Southwest Kimberley, Western Australia

In Northern Kimberley, and indeed also in East Kimberley and across to the Roper River in the Northern Territory, the making of medicine men is associated with the rainbow snake.[9] In the southwest of the Kimberley Division, however, that is, in Dampier Land and the lower Fitzroy River region, medicine men are made by spirit beings called *rai*. These are spirits of the dead, though rai are also pre-existent spirit children, including those who will be reincarnated. The rai give postulants new insides, magic stones (maban), the "inner" eye by which they will see what is normally invisible, and the "aerial or astral rope" with which they will be able to travel through the air or under the ground. Thus, they will be endowed with the occult powers of the rai.

An account, the only one, of medicine men and their making, recorded on tape by an Aborigine in his own language, has been published. Mowaldjali, a very knowledgeable Ungarinyin (Ngarinjin) man, talked freely about the subject without questions or other interruptions. As he had lived in close association with Bardi tribespeople for ten years and more, he spoke about Bardi medicine men in particular.[10]

The type of person the rai bring back to their home, "the chasm where they go in and out," to make a banman is discreet, poised, and firm; he is not a troublemaker but has good sense and is trusted by the rai. There they cut him up and hang up his insides (intestines, heart, lungs, liver, kidneys). His body is dead, but his soul remains there, and on the order of the rai to look steadily at the part hanging up, he recognizes them. His body is put over a hot earth-oven, with magic cooking stones in it, and covered with paper-bark. The perspiration streams down. The rai then replace his insides and close up the flesh. He is told that he can henceforth travel in the air like a bird or under the ground like a goanna. Actually, he is sleeping in one place while traveling in his mind, for "his spirit became many."

The rai take him and teach him many things, and magic stones change him. Some are put into his insides through the navel, and some are driven in just where the "eye muscles are connected to the ear"; these are seen flickering right in the eye. The rai dip him in a water place "like in the river," and then they put in him an "inner eye" of magic. With this he can see a long distance, as through a gap in the hills, and tell what or who is there; with it, too, he can see right through the bodies of sick people, for "the skin and the body and the flesh" appear to have many holes. The different organs have each their own color, and if they are diseased or injured their colors are changed. These "experts" with the inner eye can see "the country underneath" and can hear the spirits of the dead talking to them. Moreover, as these spirits, these rai, follow the astral (aerial) rope, so the men of high degree, the experts, alone see them and the rope and follow it. Indeed, a rai takes the new medicine man about on the aerial rope. If the rope breaks, it must be mended, for the rai never lets him go.

Mowaldjali does not say whether all the foregoing experience was in a single dream or trance or in several. But he does imply that an aspirant lets one or more of the craft know that he would like to become a doctor-man. If accepted, he would be told solemnly what to expect and the meaning of what happens. This instruction includes what to do if other medicine men chase the new "graduate" in a dream because he or some of his relations cause trouble over a bull-roarer or other matters. He is warned of the traps, especially of the opening tree that closes on him if he enters it and causes him to be sick. All this is done by a rai magician as a lesson. He opens the tree to release the one who is squeezed in it. He tells the latter to fire magic stones at the tree and to go around it; otherwise, if caught in it, he would die and go to Dulugun, the place of the dead.

In all this dream or trance experience, Mowaldjali says the trainee's mind is being "conditioned." He is being shown in his mind what to do. And by his total experience and training he is set aside, ordained, as we might say; he becomes an expert.

Such was the information about these clever men according to the accounts handed down by the old men of the tribe, said Mowaldjali. But there are no such famous men of high degree today. They and their magic stones and aerial rope belong to the times of the old identities who had complete confidence in them.

Notes

1. T. G. H. Strehlow, *Songs of Central Australia* (Sydney: Angus & Robertson, 1971), p. 261.
2. This was meant to be a chapter in a book on the Aborigines, which Mathews never finished. He obtained the material during the preceding three decades, when he spent much time in the northwest of New South Wales.
3. The Bigambul and Bandjelang material is from A. P. Elkin, Field Notes, 1946 and thereafter.
4. H. Petri, *Sterbende Welt in Nordwest-Australien*, 1954. Andreas Lommel, *Die Unambal*, 1952. Both writers referred to *Aboriginal Men of High Degree.*

5. Not far from the head of Walcott Inlet toward the junction of the Isdell River, where the water swirls, doctor-men used to dive in and get access to a subterranean cave. This was a secret place of "retreat," of meditation and visions.

   The feathers of the "crown," as Petri terms it, were those with which Unggud flew. This information comes from Bungguni, the last of the old-time doctors of the Wunambal-Woroa-Ungarinyin mixed community gathered into Mowanjum, near Derby, since 1956. I thank Mr. Howard Coate for checking my text with Bungguni.
6. Petri, *Sterbende Welt in Nordwest-Australien*, pp. 232–33. Lommel, *Die Unambal*, pp. 53–54, writes that miriru came from the dead. H. Coate, correspondence, writes that *miriru*, which is used by the Ngarinyin and also the Wunambal and Worora, is best translated as "trance."
7. Lommel, *Die Unambal*, pp. 51–52. Bungguni (see note 5) confirms that a man had to be killed and "fed" (offered) to the Unggud snake but denies that the doctors ate any of the flesh.
8. J. E. Cawte, "Tjimi and Tjagolo: Ethnopsychiatry in the Kalumburu People of North-Western Australia," *Oceania* 34 (1963–64): 170–90, especially 186–88.
9. See above; also Kaberry, *Aboriginal Woman*, pp. 213, 217. For Birrundudu in the southern part of East Kimberley, where the postulant and the native doctors fly through the air astride the rainbow snake, see R. M. and C. H. Berndt, *The World of the First Australians* (Sydney: Ure Smith, 1964), p. 257.

   In 1947, while among the Djauan and Mangarai, I learned that a clever fellow (termed *nanguranggo*) at the Elsey on the Roper River worked in the water from 6 A.M. until midday to get Bolung, the rainbow snake with two horns, out of the river. This man could "call up" spirits who would "talk" or make sounds. He was a ventriloquist and could disappear from the persons around him and talk to them as from 100 meters away (Elkin, Field Notes, 1947). Presumably, the rainbow incident was a mystic experience during the clever man's making or else a display of hypnotic power.
10. The Bardi occupied the northern tip of Dampier Land peninsula and were closely aligned with the natives of the Buccaneer Archipelago. H. H. J. Coate was responsible for this recording (made in 1964) and has published the text along with interlinear and free translations of it. "The Rai and the Third Eye," *Oceania* 38 (1966): 93–123.

CHAPTER 6

Animistic and Magical Causes of Illness

One day in 1930 near a native camp at Mount Margaret, Laverton District, Western Australia, I saw a medicine man rubbing a young man's abdomen with both hands as if gathering up an invisible something. From time to time he walked off slowly and silently about 10 meters and with his right arm hurled that "invisible something" away. The patient asked me for medicine. I gave him an aspirin. He did not doubt the medicine man's power to withdraw the cause of his pain and cure him, but in the meantime, the white man's pill would ease his pains.

Five years later, at the end of a lecture on Aboriginal medicine men to the Northern Medical Association of New South Wales,[1] some of the audience related their puzzling experiences of apparently curing Aboriginal (actually part-Aboriginal) patients of appendicitis, pneumonia, and other afflictions, and yet those patients did not make normal progress. I suggested that in the patients' view the physicians and surgeons got rid of the symptoms only, that is, the bad appendix, the congestion, and so on. They needed assurance that the "object" or "agent" that caused the bad appendix or the congestion had been drawn out. In their belief, this prior cause was magical or animistic and had been projected into them by man or spirit. Therefore, it could be removed only by their own medicine man, who through his making had been endowed with knowledge of, and power and expertise associated with, the sphere of magic and animism, of ritual and belief. Accordingly, by visible actions, expected and understood, often by producing an outward symbol or form of the invisible "prior" cause, he imparted to the patient confidence and assurance of recovery.

For this reason, too, about the same time, Aborigines in a Sydney suburb, New South Wales, met the cost of bringing a medicine man from the midwest of the state to cure a sick person. Their faith was in him, not in the skill of the white physicians. He knew the magical and mystical context of illness and cure and would act within it. Centuries of belief and ritual had made up this context.

Back in 1825, James Dunlop, the New South Wales government astronomer, recorded that a man *dreamed* that he had been speared through the body and had died. When he woke up, believing in the reality of dreams, he told Mr. Dunlop he was going to die and asked for some water, which he poured over his own head. Next day, Mr. Dunlop found him very ill and dying.[2] He had already chosen the spot where he would die and where he should be buried. Some days later, as a result of taking no food, he was indeed dying. Two sorcerers (medicine men) attended him. He was tumbled headfirst into a nearby stream, taken out and rolled in the sand, which was then washed off him. A cord was tied around his body, with the knot placed over the spot where the spear of his dream had entered. A "thread" from the knot was drawn by a young woman back and forth across her gums until she began to spit blood—blood that was said to come from the dying man's side. A swelling had risen (unaccountably, wrote Mr. Dunlop) under the knot, and a medicine man stroked the man's flesh from all directions toward this "as though to force the blood thither." He then sucked the spot and also pressed it violently with his hands until a spear point, four inches in length, "came out." He sucked again and "appeared to draw blood and corrupt matter," though there was no visible wound. Crossing the stream he threw this away. The patient, according to Mr. Dunlop, believed he would not get well, but when Mr. Dunlop sent him some tea, he would not drink it but asked that it be given to the medicine man, for if the latter drank it, he the patient would benefit. However, he died. Apparently, his death had been revealed in his dream as a fact, and not even the medicine man could prevent it. Its cause was animistic, though we might diagnose self-imposed starvation following a vivid nightmare.[3]

In 1927, just over one hundred years later, on my arrival in Broome, northwestern Australia, I heard that a Worora tribesman from 480 kilometers farther north had been brought down to Broome and put into hospital, where, in spite of medical care, he died. A postmortem revealed no cause of death. He had been "sung." Some months later I learned from the missionary in Worora country that he had seen a group of men "singing," two men who had broken marriage rules. They sang for hours with great vehemence and every now and then dug the handle-ends of their spear-throwers into the ground as though into the bodies of their intended victims. One of the latter took no notice of the "singing," with its implied sentence of death, but the other died in Broome hospital, as I have mentioned. Both men had been within the influence of the Worora Mission. The one who "took no notice" possibly had such strong backing in the tribe, ensuring revenge in case of his death, that he could ignore the singing. Or he may have been an outstanding warrior. In some cases of such magical failure, the intended victim was led into ambush and speared.

Generally speaking, a person who was sung by the elders for an offense could not recover unless those elders "withdrew" the "magical charge." In a case at Karandji (Northern Kimberley), about 1938, a woman had been sung for incest. She was terrified, and "her eyes were sunken," but when the elders thought she had been punished enough, a "doctor" saved her. Some years later, a man was sung at Yuendumu Aboriginal Settlement, northwest of Alice Springs. He, too, was terrified; he would "take" a spear through the thigh or any other punishment rather than be sung. Mr. H. Coate, the officer to whom he had told his story, saw the old men, who assured him the sung man would not die. They wanted to frighten him. Later on they lifted the "curse," after which he went into exile in the bush for a period.

In 1956 an Aboriginal young man named Wulumu was brought into Darwin Hospital from Yirrkala (in northeast Arnhem Land), unable to eat or speak. Tarlton Rayment, medical officer in charge of the case, understood that the man had been sung following a killing for which he was held responsible; he was then poisoned by his mother-in-law. "The poison picked out the respiratory center in the medulla and disturbed the swallowing mechanism." He sent me (April 17, 1956) some grass and also a mixture made from pounding up this grass, which was put in a waterhole to paralyze fish so that they were easily caught. The native had actually chewed up grass, which he passed in his feces after coming into hospital. Officers of the Division of Animal Health and Production of the Commonwealth Scientific and Industrial Research Organization experimented with both the grass and the mixture but found that goldfish, two rats, and two guinea pigs showed no adverse effects. The grass and the mixture had been flown from Yirrkala and immediately on to me in Sydney. By April 17 Wulumu was showing signs of recovery. He could stay with the respirator off for about twenty minutes each hour, and with a gastrostomy tube his nutrition was improving, but he could not swallow food, though his power of speech had returned. In time he recovered and went back to his people. This was a rare victory over both magical singing and the belief that a person had been poisoned by a "magical substance," in which recovery was at least aided by hospital ministration.[4]

Waipuldanya, who became a trained medical assistant, a black "doctor-whitefellow," had, like Wulumu, been sung to death and saved. In his case, however, he was reprieved not by a white doctor and hospital treatment but by a doctor-blackfellow. He was sung possibly for a ritual error made by another member of his cult group. He became suddenly ill, and his grandfather solemnly pronounced that he had been sung. Only a powerful medicine man could save him. Doctor blackfellow Gudjiwa was called. He stuffed an herbal mixture down Waipuldanya's throat, performed an energetic dance around him, then put his hand over the boy's heart, and sucked his arm near the shoulder. "In a moment he spat a mouthful of blood" into a bark dish and repeated this until the dish was dripping with blood. Gudjiwa then rubbed bushes over the boy's chest and, with a final mouthful of blood, spat out "a red star-shaped shell." Instantly, the boy began to improve and in a week was quite well.

Waipuldanya was not conscious of the medicine man's treatment, but learned about it from his grandfather. He was satisfied, even after receiving his medical training, that Gudjiwa got the blood by sucking it through his skin. He argued that Gudjiwa could not have had it in his mouth before the sucking process, because he was chanting and opening his mouth wide and, when sucking, emptied his mouth more than once. Waipuldanya did not mention the possibility that the medicine man might have cut his own lips or gum with the small star-shaped shell that was in his mouth. But he did concede that it might have been a trick, "an exceptionally clever one." In any case, he was convinced that bad blood was removed, and he did get better.[5]

Black and White Medicine: Parallel and Complementary

The Aborigines had their traditional pattern of diagnosis and treatment of sickness. Kinsfolk as in duty bound looked after the sick, providing the accustomed remedies. If the affliction didn't yield or if it were judged to be serious, possibly caused by sorcery or by the spirits, a doctor-man took over. This pattern of diagnosis and treatment was continued after white settlers, missions, and government agencies gave some attention to what they regarded as the Aborigines' medical needs. They handed out medicine, blankets, and bandages. Nurses or other kindly disposed persons, and occasionally a physician, visited them in their camps.

This meager Western treatment did not disturb traditional routine. The two went along parallel lines and no doubt sometimes fortuitously complemented each other to the greater benefit of the patient. In any case the medicine man was the only diagnostician and healer in whom the Aborigines had faith.

The later provision of "hospitals" with a few beds for supervised treatment and to get patients off the ground did not change this situation, at least not in communities where the traditional social and psychological context had not been fundamentally changed. This context, however, remains an operative factor in Aboriginal life long after the nomadic food-gathering and hunting economy has been discarded. Nearly forty years ago, I recorded an illustration of this in a hospital for a large Aboriginal and part-Aboriginal community in southeast Queensland. It was run by a matron of understanding, nursing staff, and visiting medical officer. In one way or another, patients' relations smuggled in to them their accustomed food (irrespective of the diet they should be on) and traditional "medicines," including liniments such as goanna fat mixed with other ingredients, which were rubbed on the patient's body and came off on the clean white sheets. A medicine man also made his way in and ministered to "the faithful." Such incursions were regarded as inevitable, especially when older people were concerned. Thus patients received, to their content, independent, parallel treatments from two cultural sources, which in them became complementary, even if not planned as such by matron and physician.

During fieldwork in 1953–54 among the Wailbri (Walbiri) at Hooker Creek Aboriginal Settlement, northwest Central Australia, M. J. Meggitt observed a similar twofold approach to their ills. Ordinary indispositions that seemingly come on suddenly, such as influenza, earache, migraine, and so on, were treated in a bicultural way. They were attributed to malevolent, spiritual beings, the *Djanba,* who put "something" in the sick person during the preceding night. The medicine man's standard treatment consisted of removing the something from the afflicted person by inserting *mabanba* (magic stones) into, and sucking, the affected part, and by softly chanting over the victim to ensure that the something would recoil from him to the Djanba. The patient would then try the white man's medicine at the sick bay. The psychological effect of the former treatment and the physiological effect of the latter usually resulted in a quick recovery. Most, if not all, of the credit went to the medicine man.

In these or other cases in which the usual procedure failed to give relief, the medicine man realized that the Djanba had taken some portion of the patient's body, which he must recover. To do this he went into a "state of deep contemplation, perhaps even of trance," sent out his familiar, a small, nonmaterial lizard, to locate the thieving Djanba, "fired" his mabanba at the latter, who, if hit, released the missing part of the patient's body. It returned automatically to its place in the latter and recovery followed quickly. If the magic stones missed the Djanba, the patient died.[6]

Such complementary "black and white" treatment of illnesses was customary in the 1960s, and may still be so, at Jigalong Mission, over 1,000 kilometers to the west of the Walbiri. The mission was established in 1946 in the western fringe of the Gibson Desert, and about 480 kilometers from the Western Australian coast. Several inland tribal groups and remnants, including a couple from the desert, gravitated to it. The population, averaging about 300, included "approximately fifteen" native doctors. This relatively large number of professionals at one settlement probably reflects the wise separation of groups in the arid and desert conditions from which they migrated. It also expressed the felt need of such groups for readily available psychic and bodily "help in time of trouble."

The doctor-men had maban (magical substances of power) inside them and in most cases spirit-familiars, also. They were able to see inside people and so to diagnose illness. Moreover, they practiced all the usual techniques, physical, psychological, and make-believe. And according to Dr. Tonkinson, who did anthropological research at Jigalong on several occasions in the 1960s, they had not lost any of "their clientele" to the mission clinic, which was run by a trained nurse, although the Aborigines eagerly accepted all forms of medicine, especially injections. They regarded them, however, as only supplementary to the treatment by their own doctor-men.[7]

Dr. Tonkinson does not refer to the making of medicine men except to say that most of them "inherit their special powers from their fathers," that is, from "the spirits of their dead patrilineal forebears" and their ancestral totemic beings who live under Lake Disappointment, and with whom they must keep in effective communication. Some of the powers attributed to them, however, suggest that they were made in a mystic experience that included visitation by spirits and receiving maban inside them. These powers include being leaders on dream-spirit journeys, especially those associated with the religious life, taking persons' dream spirits on a journey by sitting them astride lengths of hair-string, or if men only, astride of sacred boards, vehicles that the doctors create by blowing on their maban stones,[8] and protecting people "against attacks by malignant spirits."

Doctor-Man in Health Services

By the 1970s, some Europeans concerned with the provision of health services for Aborigines were recognizing that medicine men had an essential role to play. Their cooperation in Central Australia was sought and gained in several centers by medical officers from Alice Springs. Visiting the groups, they asked through the older men whether they would like their traditional healers to work in their settlement health centers with the medical sisters. A research linguist helped with the inquiries in one group, the Pintubi, and a missionary linguist in the Walbiri groups. By the end of 1971 two Pintubi medicine men were working as liaison "officers" with their own people in the camp and as helpers at the Papunya Settlement clinic, 257 kilometers west of Alice Springs. Pintubi groups had migrated to Papunya since the mid-1950s from their own territory over 150 kilometers west of Papunya. Early in 1973, they moved back 40 to 50 kilometers to Yaiyai Bore accompanied by their two medicine men. Supplied with a chest of medicines and bandages and with supplementary foods in tins for babies and nursing mothers, they worked well and responsibly. The Yaiyai community responded favorably.

The replacement in the clinic for these two medicine men by the people remaining at Papunya, mostly Ngalia (Walbiri speakers), took some time. Discussions between them and the medical officers in September-October 1973 seemed to get nowhere. But many months later some Aboriginal councilors, when talking to one of the officers about another matter, suddenly said, "We have the two men . . . the ones you were talking about—the *watingengkari* [the doctor-men] for the hospital—they are ready now."

At Yuendumu, 290 kilometers northwest of Alice Springs and in Walbiri territory, similar talks between medical officers and Aboriginal leaders in February 1973, and in May with some doctor-men, resulted in two of the latter working at the clinic. They were not satisfactory because they were too old to adapt themselves to clinic procedures. The missionary linguist and the medical officers thought that the elders had selected these two old men deliberately because they were not sure of the official intentions. However, after further consultation in July, a very good medicine man who was practicing in the camp unknown to the clinic sisters and the superintendent of the settlement agreed to be involved in the clinic work and has proved very satisfactory.

In this same year, 1973, two medicine men were cooperating well in the hospital clinic at Warrabri Settlement, near Tennant Creek.[9]

Although Aboriginal leaders and healers were somewhat hesitant about accepting the invitation to become involved in the official health services, the experiment was successful in the period 1971–75. And it was so because they realized that the official health officers did not appreciate the Aborigines' approach to, and understanding of, the causes of illness and death, and that therefore the help of their own medicine men was necessary.

An important and significant example of this cooperation comes from Yuendumu. In the mid-1970s, the hospital with its sick bay had an elderly Aboriginal nursing aide who was also a medicine man in whom the people had great faith. He practiced his own native skills such as sucking, massaging, and withdrawing substances but in conjunction with the precautions and techniques he learned as a hospital assistant.

A linguist at Yuendumu has kindly given me the following information (in correspondence, June 1976) about her own experience toward the end of 1975. Two carbuncles between the third and fourth fingers of one hand, and the consequent swelling of the hand and forearm, caused a week of agony, which antibiotics and painkillers failed to relieve. On the entreaty of Aboriginal friends, she agreed to let the doctor-man look at it. He did so in a very professional manner. She then agreed to his request to suck the hand, hoping at least for relief of the intense pain. Turning the palm downward, he sucked the back of the hand "where the veins run that go between the knuckles." After about thirty seconds she felt that something was coming out of her hand, and when he took his mouth away, he spat out blood and pus into some tissues. He repeated the process twice, giving relief as the pressure decreased. At the third sucking he produced a *yarda*; it looked like a small piece of pointed quartz, but she did not see it or the blood come out, nor any perforations on her hand. Her hand felt better for about an hour. Then the pressure and pain built up again. The medicine man repeated the sucking on the next two days, an absolutely painless process, and spat out blood and pus each time—but not yarda. He then said he could do no more until he could take out the cores, but the rest of the pus began to be released within twenty-four hours of the third sucking. Two days after this he extracted the cores and then dressed the wound daily. Later on he massaged the hand to remove the stiffness.

This white person benefited from the knowledge and skills of two cultures, on the one hand taking antibiotics from the hospital sister and on the other hand receiving indigenous treatment from the doctor-man, almost in parallel fashion. In the doctor-man, however, the two traditions were complementary.[10]

Not only full-blood Aborigines recently removed from their own traditional way of life, but also great numbers of "advanced" Aborigines, including part-Aborigines, still attribute illnesses and deaths (except possibly of the very old) to magical practices, to the activities of spirits, usually spirits of the departed, and to breaking taboos.[11] The age-old philosophy of life in all its phases has not been superseded by European explanations and theories of conception, illness, and death.

This is the case, for example, in the Northwest Division of Western Australia in spite of over a century of pastoral occupation in the coastal region and of about seventy years inland to the fringe of the desert, and in spite also of recent intensive metal mining. The large Aboriginal population retains to this day traditional views on the causes of sickness and death and relies on medicine men to deal with the former, especially at the point where the white doctors and hospitals fail.

A recent example (January 1976) of this and of complementary, bicultural treatment comes from the Carnarvon district, Western Australia. While hunting, a young Aboriginal stationhand believed he saw a "feather-foot" (Kadaitja) man.[12] Terrified, he fled into the bush. The local branch of the Community Health Department sent out an Aboriginal assistant, who fortunately was a medicine man, to bring him in. The assistant is said to have sung chants, "calling on spirits of the young man's ancestors to help him fight the feather-foot man." This happened, and he calmed down. He was brought into the hospital, where he recovered quickly. The hospital physicians attributed the young fellow's disturbance to the psychological effects on him of "the recent deaths of his mother and a close friend." The people on the Aboriginal reserve, however, saw the cause in the feather-foot man and thought of bringing down from Port Hedland a powerful doctor-man "to look at him."[13]

The difficulty in many regions today is to find "doctors" who are "men of high degree," who have not only learned the ritual and manipulative actions they should perform, but also have had the spiritual experience that gives them the strong or inner eye, the addition of magical "substances" to their "insides," and the assistance of personal totems. The depth of their knowledge and the essence of their power lie in this experience. They have been through great fear and even "death" and can impart confidence to those who face similar trials.

Men of High Degree: Their Passing?

The Order of Men of High Degree together with the belief in associated psychic, psychological, and physical aspects of its members' "making and powers" has seemed to many observers doomed to pass away as Aborigines accept Western ideas of illness, its cause and cure. In the meantime, the doctors of the Order could function usefully in a changing Aboriginal society. The decline in the number and activities of doctor-men has been an inevitable consequence of the white man's occupation and exploitation of the Aborigines' land, wherever it was of economic value. Depopulation followed rapidly, along with dispersal of remnants on the fringes of townships, on pastoral properties, and on missions or other organized settlements. In this process of depopulation and dispersal indigenous culture was undermined and with it the context of human needs and beliefs to and in which men of high degree are the response, that is, have their rationale.

The few elderly, part-Aboriginal clever fellows in widely separated parts of New South Wales whom I and some others either knew or were told about in the course of field research from two to four decades ago were lone survivors amid cultural wrecks. So, too, W. E. H. Stanner reported that only one *miumdakar* doctor-blackfellow "remained in 1932 amongst all the tribes" or tribal remnants on the Daly River, south of Darwin, and he was only "a little bit" miumdakar.[14]

Similarly, among the Wunambal, Worora, and Ungarinyin of Northern Kimberley, Western Australia, at Mowanjum, near Derby, where most of them now live, there is only one doctor-man, and he is only "a little bit doctor."[15]

At Kalumburu Mission, in the far north of Northern Kimberley, where the seven original tribes of the area served by the mission have settled, there were in 1963 six surviving doctor-men, elderly men whose secrets will be lost with their death.[16] And in the Gunwinggu and neighboring tribes of western Arnhem Land "by the late 1940s and 1950s, fewer than a dozen middling- to high-powered living 'clever men' could be identified," though "a larger fringe of men" were considered to have "a little" power, and that not always certain. By 1966, however, "almost all of the more easily identified 'clever men' were dead," and the number of "marginal ones" was diminishing.[17]

In Central Australia Doctors J. E. Cawte and M. A. Kidson concluded from field inquiries in 1964 that medicine men were decreasing in number at Yuendumu, 290 kilometers northwest of Alice Springs. This was in spite of the rapid increase of population there, from 350 to 700 in ten years.[18] And as mentioned above (p. 142) Professor Strehlow considered that the last Western Aranda man of high degree died in the mid-1960s.

The Desert: A Rampart for Indigenous Culture

Southwest of the Aranda and their immediate neighbors, however, the arid environment delayed and for the most part prevented white occupation of tribal lands and, also, until the late 1930s, missionary penetration. As a result, cultural integration was maintained by an adequate population, made up of an arc-like series of tribes, possessing the same social organization and pattern of beliefs and ritual and speaking dialects of a common language. They extended from the Everard and Musgrave ranges in the northwest of South Australia and around and across the corner where that state, the Northern Territory, and Western Australia meet. Moreover, this cultural heritage was retained in spite of migration of local groups east and southeast and even south across the Great Victorian Desert, forced out by very long droughts and attracted by the apparent advantages of conditions created by white settlement.[19]

The most widespread and widespreading of the tribes in that southwest arc in 1930 and since was the Pidjandja-djara, moving out from the Petermann, Mann, and other ranges in that corner region, as from a perennial human spring.[20]

This persisting indigenous culture included the medicine-man complex. Indeed, it was not under any attack even after the founding of Ernabella Mission in 1937 and of ration depots (later government Aboriginal settlements) at Haasts Bluff in 1940 and Areyonga in 1943. Pidjandja-djara were attracted to all three. Others drifted east, for example, to Angus

Downs. In all of them European medicines and treatment were accepted, but not to the exclusion of the essential treatment given by their own medicine men. An average of three hundred Pidjandja-djara were at Areyonga in the 1950s. In June 1953 I witnessed at night a very important and stirring Petermann Range "historical" ritual 6 kilometers from the settlement. In spite of settlement organization and employment and in spite of missionary endeavors, belief and ritual were still strong and influential.

In 1952, 150 Pidjandja-djara at Angus Downs, east of Ayers Rock, included one doctor-man. He had a small black stone that he sucked out of his patients' stomachs or foreheads. His services were still in demand although the group had been visited for nineteen years by European medical officers, and although both he and others asked the anthropologist for tablets for minor ailments.[21]

The number of doctor-men in the northwest corner of South Australia has not been recorded, but one or more are reported from all but very small groups. In 1975 there were three (*ngangkari*) among the thirty-three persons at Pipalyatjara in the Tomkinson Ranges. This apparent over-supply was probably a fortuitous happening in a time of decentralization and much movement.[22] The treatment consisted of massage expertly done, "followed by sucking the affected part and removing 'bad blood' and . . . the foreign object" (generally a nondescript piece of wood). This treatment was the same in other Pidjandja-djara groups and among the Janggundjara (at Everard Park). As elsewhere, too, the sick willingly accepted and usually asked for tablets, eye drops, and other simple remedies.[23]

We have already seen that to the north of the Aranda, medicine men are still functioning among the Walbiri in northwest Central Australia and also in the Northwest Division of Western Australia among the groups in the Carnarvon and Port Hedland coastal districts and inland at Jigalong. The vast arid and desert environments separating Central Australia from Western Australia's Northwest Division have thwarted European settlement and thereby delayed the collapse of indigenous institutions, including the Order of Men of High Degree. The breakdown of the Order, however, as it functioned before contact, seems inevitable.

Western influences are all-pervasive. Missions provide spiritual interpretations and ministrations; educational and medical services teach and practice our understanding of sickness and death; and, in our opinion, the marvels of modern technology must surely outdo the wonders of the clever men; we think of telephone, wireless, television, and X-ray, of gramophones and tape recorders, of trains, motors, airplanes, and space vehicles.

In the Aborigines' opinion, however, all this knowledge and all the beneficial activities of priests, teachers, physicians, and technologists are manifestations or developments in the white man's world of what the Aboriginal clever men know and do, or did, in their world. The doctor-blackfellow cures the sick or finds a reason why he fails to do so; the Flying Doctor and the wireless are marvelous in our eyes, but the medicine man by means of his cord or through the help of his totem or spirit-familiar can send word through the air with the speed of thought—"all a same wireless"; moreover, the actuality of dreams, the personal experience of dreams, is more significant than the picture on the television screen; and the penetrating power of the inner or strong eye enables the medicine man to see directly the condition of a sick person's insides without an X-ray machine and electric power. So, too, the extraction of magical objects and bad blood or other matter from his insides by rubbing, sucking, sleight of hand, and other ritual acts is in line with our surgeon's use of the knife to remove whatever is causing the trouble and pain.

A New Type: Blackfellow-Doctor-Whitefellow

Eventually, however, in the contact situation the medicine man's knowledge and skill are inadequate for dealing with some sicknesses, and finding magical or animistic explanations of failure does not satisfy. This is illustrated in the experience of Waipuldanya (Phillip Roberts), a full-blood of the Alawa tribe, lower Roper River, Northern Territory. Brought up on the mission there and well trained by white medical officers to be a medical assistant, he was on duty at Maningrida Settlement and Liverpool River district, northern Arnhem Land. He confronted a doctor-blackfellow, Malagwia, the most powerful one on that part of the coast, whose only son was very sick with a poisoned foot. Malagwia admitted that he could not cure the boy himself but refused to bring him to Waipuldanya, because he, a doctor-blackfellow, would be seen seeking treatment from a blackfellow who was trained as a "doctor-whitefellow." So the latter went to Malagwia's camp, for that would not shame him.

Replying to his question about the hypodermic syringe, Waipuldanya (through an interpreter) answered diplomatically, "Proper doctor-blackfellow magic. If I inject this fluid [it was penicillin] into your son, it will force out the devil that is inside his leg and killing him." Malagwia was satisfied, and when his wife began to cry as the needle was pushed in, he said, "Can't you see that a doctor-blackfellow . . . one of my colleagues . . . is trying to cure your son?" But Waipuldanya said, "I'm not a doctor-blackfellow," to which Malagwia retorted, "You-ai! Proper doctor-blackfellow," and when Waipuldanya was finished and stood up, the other held him by the shoulders in "fraternal greeting—the intimate acknowledgement of equals." What is more, he agreed to bring the boy for several days to the clinic where, said Waipuldanya, "I am a more powerful singer."

Seeing that his son was cured, the old man asked Waipuldanya to treat himself and his wife for some eruptions on their legs and arms. When these disappeared, he went to Waipuldanya and "bestowed the ultimate accolade": "Doctor . . . ," he said fervently, "Doctor. . . ." "I was overcome," said Waipuldanya, for "I could not doubt that his people regarded him almost as a Dreaming in whom they believed blindly." But he could not cure his son, his wife, or himself with his own mixtures and magic. He allowed a new kind of medicine man, a blackfellow with white man's medical skill, to treat the three of them with "other drugs . . . taken from herbs and bushes and bark and Mould."[24] This new type of blackfellow-doctor blended his skill and knowledge into indigenous understanding and practice, and so could be recognized by the old-time doctor-blackfellow. That was "professional" recognition within an Aboriginal cultural context.

The following incident was patient-doctor recognition in a cross-cultural situation. Waipuldanya, on medical walkabout in 1958 along with a hunting group, came across ten Navy men surveying the estuary of the Cadell River, northern Arnhem Land. When the Navy men overcame their astonishment on learning that this Aboriginal hunter was a qualified medical assistant, they, on their request, were treated by Waipuldanya for dysentery, sores, and various aches with sulphadiazine and other items from his medical kit. Their respect for him became obvious: black skin, but doctor-whitefellow.[25]

Cross-cultural patient-doctor recognition was also involved in the case at Yuendumu, northwest of Alice Springs, to which I have referred (p. 164). But in it, the local medicine man, who was also a hospital assistant, treated the patient, a white woman, biculturally. Although her understanding of the cause of the carbuncles and their distressful sequence was probably very different from his—a cultural world apart—she had confidence in the indigenous method of removing that cause as he understood it. But he also carried out the white doctor's treatment for extracting the cores of the carbuncles. He was blackfellow-doctor-whitefellow.

Significantly, Waipuldanya was not himself a man of high degree, and yet Malagwia, who was one, recognized him as doctor-blackfellow. He was, however, a fully initiated man; he was a member of the "high cults" of the region, the Yabuduruwa and Kunapipi; and he had passed through an actual experience of being sung and on the verge of physical death, and then being saved, made alive, by a man of high degree. This suggests the possibility of Aboriginal men of character and understanding, if fully initiated and bearing in themselves their people's culture, being recognized as blackfellow-doctor-whitefellow, provided they have been trained in the white man's medicine. But if the person so trained were a known man of high degree, then he would indeed be a blackfellow-doctor-whitefellow. In him the indigenous "medical" heritage would take into itself the white man's medical heritage and thereby gain greater health-giving potential.

Such persons would be qualified to educate their communities in health measures such as hygiene and diet and to appreciate the medical treatment given by non-Aboriginal doctors, without forsaking useful folk medicines and without losing respect for their own medicine men.[26]

In these present years of rapid change in which Aborigines are developing their own communities, with official encouragement and help, white authorities feel constrained to consider the Aborigines' own approach to sickness and injuries when planning health services for such communities. Much of their sickness and below-standard health has resulted from white contact and particularly from the changes from nomadic to sedentary life and from naturally gathered foods to purchased foodstuffs. In this program, community hospital, trained nurse, and medical officer are basic. But to station fully qualified western-type physicians in those many scattered communities is impossible and for two reasons is unnecessary. First, radio and airplane make their advice and presence available to the local staff. The second is the cooperation, if obtainable, of the medicine man with the community health service as consultant and also as a nursing aide or better still as a trained medical assistant. An important aspect is the mutual recognition by the non-Aboriginal doctor and hospital sister on the one hand and by the Aboriginal doctor-man on the other hand, of their complementary roles in ministering to the health of the community. The gulf between them is culturally wide and historically deep. The approach of one is mainly biological and physical; the other's approach is mainly psychological and animistic. Moreover, the Aboriginal medicine man is himself a product and bearer of the culture of which that psychological makeup and that body of psychic and animistic beliefs are an integral part.

An experienced and proven medicine man is not likely to become a fully qualified medical practitioner; his lack of secondary and possibly also of primary education would be an almost insuperable barrier to matriculation and university work. Eventually, there will be qualified Aboriginal medical practitioners educated from their teens to be such. But the long absences from their own tribal or other groups, possibly while at secondary school and certainly at a distant university receiving education and training primarily designed for life as Europeans, could result in loss of cultural Aboriginality. They might become estranged from the social and psychological conditions and values of their own people, and so would have lost the advantage of the medicine men in health work among their people. However, if they had been initiated, preferably before entering university or during a long vacation, and had been admitted to some important rituals, this risk would be lessened. In any case, a course on the social and cultural anthropology of the Aborigines should be included in their academic training. Indeed, their university education might be given more appropriately in the University of Papua New Guinea, where the emphasis is on the medical and health needs of an emergent people.[27]

Medicine Men: The Psychotherapeutic Role

The decline in the number of men of high degree throughout the decades of racial and cultural contact, until in some regions they are barely a memory, has been unfortunate. Missionaries and other bearers of civilization to the Aborigines, convinced that Western health services were superior to indigenous methods, especially for coping with introduced diseases, tended, at least until recently, to ignore or brush aside the doctor-men. The latter, however, were and are the family doctors of their people, and through them, through their cooperation, faith in modern health services could develop more readily than by exhortation and imposition from without.[28] Moreover, they could help their people to cope with the strains and anxieties resulting from contact, as well as those arising from the ups and downs of life. These are not idle words, for the true doctor-men impart a sense of power and confidence. The psychiatrist Dr. J. E. Cawte wrote, as a result of a field study among full-bloods in far northwest Australia: "If faith and hope are healing emotions, the *Punmun* [medicine man] mobilizes them as do psychotherapists in other cultures" and does so by using "elements common to all psychotherapeutic systems" together with the scientific knowledge available in his culture. Dr. Cawte, however, does not see any continuing role for native doctor-men in the context of social disintegration. In his *Medicine is the Law* (1974), especially in the chapters "The Exceptional Family," "The Sick Society," and "Casualties of Change," he discusses the maladaption and maladjustment of Aborigines that arise in the process of alien contact. He then suggests that the modern medical practitioner should become a nucleus for social integration, thus replacing the doctor-man.[29]

Medicine Men and the Invisible

In Aboriginal thought, man is twofold. He is visible body, but he is also spirit. The latter is invisible except to those with special sight. Moreover, it is with the spiritual phenomena that the doctor-man's specialty lies. He works with and through the invisible: for example, drawing out from a patient's body an "invisible something," which he casts away; reading a person's thoughts whether he be nearby or out of sight and far away; practicing meditation, clairvoyance, telepathy, and hypnotism; sending his assistant spirit or totem to gather information; and, in trance and dream, visiting the spirits of the dead, of nature, and of the sky-world.

To specialize in the invisible aspect of man's life, and in the sphere of spirit generally, a person must be "made," that is, transformed, and so qualified. Aborigines are familiar with the concept of qualifying for status and role. Every man must pass through the several psychological and physical tests of initiation to be "made man" and a full member of the tribe. Ritual headmen have had to learn the myths, chants, symbols, and acted scenes from, and under the supervision of, "past masters."

Likewise, as we have seen, the would-be man of high degree must qualify for his role in the tribe. So he "takes" the high degree. Apart from being expert in folk remedies, he must know how to deal with fears and anxieties, as well as physical illnesses, even if he uses what may seem to be conjuror's tricks. Thus, massaging and sucking the skin may in fact tone up the area treated and relieve pain, but, more important, they are the preliminary part of a sacramental rite; the "bad blood," the animistic "badness," and the material object that is apparently extracted are the outward signs that the cause of pain, illness, and anxiety has been taken away.

Effective performance of symbolic acts that heal and cure flow from the psychic power received by the doctor-man in his own prior mystic experience as a postulant. He is told by his mentor or mentors what to expect, and in "retreat," in isolation and fasting, he ponders somewhat fearfully at the edge of the spirit world about what will happen. At length, be it in dream or trance, he believes that he is visited by a sky cult-being, by spirits of the dead, or by a nature spirit. Thus, he is made. He receives the inner eye and new insides or "something in him" that mediates power from the spirit world.

The Order: Resurgence

The widespread decline of medicine men to which I have referred was reported during the 1960s to be happening in still other regions, but the picture is changing. When Cawte and Kidson concluded from their field inquiries that decline was occurring at Yuendumu in 1964, they understood that new "doctors" were "not being trained to any extent," and at least half of the doctor-men whom they questioned attributed this decline to loss of potency in their *mabanba*.[30] These psychiatrists' conclusions, however, have not been entirely borne out.

On the one hand, of the eight adult medicine men whom they named and consulted, only two were on a list sent to me by Dr. Dayalan Devanesen of the Northern Territory Health Department in July 1976; but as against that fact, twelve others were on it, making fourteen for the community. Six dropped out. Likewise, although the last Western Aranda medicine man was thought to have died in the middle 1960s (p.142), two doctor-men of that subtribe were said to have "excellent practices" in 1976.

In that year, too, ten medicine men were listed in Papunya Settlement and five more at three other small centers, as well as four women healers at Papunya, and lists have still to be made for other places in Central Australia where doctor-men have made their presence known recently.[31]

A significant factor must have come into being sometime after 1964 to explain why thirty-one medicine men have come forward in the region from Hermannsburg north to Yuendumu, and others elsewhere in Central Australia, willing to consult with and in some ways to cooperate with the Department of Health. That factor was the department's recognition of medicine men as, at this stage at least, essential to its Aboriginal health services. Apparently, most tribal healers had remained in the background, but in the last few years many have responded to the medical officers' requests for discussion and help.

Whether all these healers are men of high degree, like their fellow doctor-men elsewhere in Australia, has not been revealed. Cawte and Kidson, referring to Yuendumu, wrote in 1964 that a doctor depends on possessing mabanba, and this he usually inherits. He is trained by his father, but there are "not complex rites and ordeals through which the novitiate doctor had to pass."[32] As these investigators had only four weeks at that settlement, and also had to employ interpreters, they were handicapped in obtaining information on the secret making. Recent inquiries have discovered that the procedure does include "mystical ceremonies," and that most medicine men claim to have extraordinary dreams and to be able to communicate with spirits. At least some experience trance and are clairvoyant. Moreover, northern Walbiri doctor-men at Hooker Creek, who send out their spirit-familiars to search for and recover a stolen part of patients' bodies, are made by bush-spirits, the *guruwalba,* suggesting a mystic experience in the making. In this, the postulant is ritually killed and is spoken to only by the guruwalba with a "subdued tongue-clicking," so as not to attract the attention of the aggressive Djanba spirits.[33]

South of Yuendumu also, a (Kukatja) doctor-man from Haasts Bluff, near Papunya, who has a hole pierced in his tongue, inherited three spirit familiars from his father. He received them while lying all day "naked in the sun," when also his soul left his body and "went on a journey." Particulars of the journey have not been recorded, but doctor-men at Jigalong, far west across the Gibson Desert, make dream-spirit journeys to keep in touch with their patrilineal ancestors who now live under Lake Disappointment (p. 162).[34]

Even if in a particular region the procedure lacked, or had lost, the normal elements of retreat, fasting, and mystic experience, the present great resurgence of tribal and intertribal rituals in Central Australia would encourage their revival. If the Aborigines there, especially the tribal healers, desired such revival, and if no one, which I would doubt, was himself qualified and experienced to direct the procedure, members of the Order from elsewhere could do so. For instance, Dr. W. E. Roth wrote in 1903 that if a postulant of the Maitakudi tribe, near Cloncurry, failed to experience the response of the nature spirit, he had to make a long journey to a Goa tribal group, where he could be put through a death and revival ritual.[35]

This was and is possible because the making and powers of men of high degree were essentially the same everywhere since first reported in the earliest years of European settlement. There are regional variations such as the role of the sky god or sky culture-hero in the east, of the rainbow snake in the west, and of spirits of the dead and of nature in Central and North-central Australia. These divisions are not precise, and if we had more information we might find more overlapping than we now know. Similarly, with medicine men's powers: for example, up to 1944, their use of cords, aerial rope, was reported only from Victoria and inland New South Wales, but since then I have recorded it for the north coast of the latter state, for the Gladstone and Cloncurry districts, respectively in coastal and far inland Queensland,"[36] and in this chapter for Dampier Land, southwest Kimberley, Western Australia. Possibly, it was also a psychic phenomenon displayed by members of the craft in tribes in between. In any case, it was only one example of occult power a clever man possessed.

But will young men of character seek making? Lamilami of the Maung tribe, Goulburn Islands, said in 1974, "None of the young men wanted to learn the things their fathers knew, because they think these things are all past now."[37] Dr. Cawte, too, gives an example of a westernized Aborigine who had no faith in the doctor-man whom he saw treating a patient but admitted that the patient got better. And the reason! "Make 'im glad, eat 'im tucker straight-away . . . from his heart he feel glad and get better." The sick man was cured by his own and the doctor-man's faith—a faith the westernized Aborigine no longer held.[38] This Aborigine, however, would himself probably consult a doctor-man if he became seriously ill and thought sorcery was involved. He would go back to the beliefs and measures of his people.

Although Aborigines appreciate what is done for them in illness, I doubt whether any of those in the first two or three and even more generations of contact, marked as they are by strain and nonacceptance in the general community, really feel that power, "virtue," passes from Western doctors to themselves. The late Mrs. Eileen Lester, M.B.E., a Western Australian Aborigine of an arid region tribe north of Laverton, was trained by the Church Army, and in recent years was a social welfare and health worker among Aborigines in New South Wales. In other words, she was westernized, educated, and a Christian. But when, extending her work in 1974 to Aboriginal women in northwest South Australia, she met the elders and leaders and took her place with the women on the periphery of rituals, she said the personality, influence, and spiritual power of those headmen were impressive—something never to be forgotten. She felt it good for her to be there. Her enthusiasm and almost veneration for the living and pulsating culture from which she had been separated for two or three decades were real and astonishing. She was "returning to the mat" and gaining contentment.[39]

Intertribal Conference of Medicine Men

In view of the growing trend toward employing medicine men in Aboriginal health services, I suggest that the Commonwealth Health Department invite up to three from each community or district to a conference. This would best be held not in a township, but at an Aboriginal settlement, possibly west or north of Alice Springs. They could be brought there from other places in the Northern Territory, including Arnhem Land, and from South and Western Australia.

The conference should be run by the medicine men themselves, but it could be joined at special sessions by some influential "old men" to represent the opinions, feelings, and reactions of various communities. In addition, a white medical officer would explain at the opening the sorts of questions the departments would like the meeting to include in its agenda. He would then retire but remain on hand for consultation and for the last session.

Such a conference, that is, such an important intertribal meeting, is not new to Aborigines. It is common in these days of Aboriginal conferences, boards, and meetings for different purposes. In the past, leaders of groups and ritual headmen met to discuss and plan important rituals both before they were held and during performances.

The business of the conference would be

1. for all present to consider the relevance of medicine men and the contributions, if any, they could make in the present phase of contact and of increasing Aboriginal self-determination; then, if a favorable opinion be reached:
2. for medicine men, being men of high degree, to discuss the ritual of making as they experienced it, and to suggest what parts, if any, should be retained or modified, e.g., the retreat with its discipline, fasting, meditation, and mystic experience; and the teaching to be given on manipulation, on the new psychology of their own people, and on psychic powers; and
3. for all present to consider the place of the medicine man, the doctor-man, in the health services, and whether he should be trained to be a medical assistant, a blackfellow-doctor-whitefellow.

Members of such a conference should understand that final decisions would not be expected from one meeting, but only after two or three meetings at intervals of a few months. Adjournments would enable them to think over and discuss the implications of possible decisions, back in and with their own communities. Only in this way would decisions be acceptable and final.

But conference or no conference, medicine men should be recognized by Western doctors and nurses for what they are: specialists in the psychology and social system of their own people and media of spiritual power to them. As a ritual headman in southern Arnhem Land told me in 1949: "White doctor *only* got clever head; blackfellow-doctor clever—got something inside."

Notes

1. A. P. Elkin, "Primitive Medicine Men," *The Medical Journal of Australia* (November 30, 1935): 750–57.
2. Mr. Dunlop added, "from fear of death." I doubt this. He was dying under what he regarded as a sentence of death from the dream world and was not afraid.
3. N. Gunson, ed., *Australian Reminiscences and Papers of L. E. Threlkeld* (Canberra: Australian Institute of Aboriginal Studies, 1974), vol. 2, appendix 4, pp. 341–42. Mr. Dunlop did not record whether the medicine man drank the tea. Unless it were cold, he would not have done so.
4. Waipuldanya (Phillip Roberts), an Alawa tribesman, was training as a medical orderly at Darwin Hospital when Wulumu was being treated by Dr. Rayment "with a mixture of white-feller medicine and his own brand of hocus-pocus." Remarkable recovery followed. Waipuldanya doesn't mention that Wulumu was sung for a killing but only for philandering, a charge made by his wife's mother. He was shown his nulla-nulla at the top of a tall tree—a sign that he had been sung to death. Within a few hours he became unconscious, Douglas Lockwood, *I, the Aboriginal* (Adelaide: Rigby, 1962), pp. 22–23. Mr. Lockwood was in Darwin at the time of this incident.

   I had suggested that the medical officer should consider calling in an Aboriginal elder. For several years a Melville Island native who lived in Darwin was always ready to visit the native ward in the hospital and for a small payment to cast out the magical cause of sickness from a patient and so prepare him for recovery when the white doctor had dealt with the symptoms.
5. Lockwood, *I, the Aboriginal*, pp. 17–20.
6. M. J. Meggitt, "Djanba among the Walbiri, Central Australia," *Anthropos* 50 (1955): 388–91. These medicine men are made by bush spirits, *guruwal balu*; indeed, that is the latters' sole function. A postulant is "found" (selected) while still a boy and while asleep, by a "dreaming" snake (not the rainbow), and during his making he receives magic "pebbles" from the spirits. Unfortunately, no other details have been published. Ibid., pp. 391, 398. A Capell, "The Walbiri through Their Own Eyes," *Oceania* 23 (1952–53): 117–19.
7. Robert Tonkinson, *The Aboriginal Victors of the Desert Crusade* (Cummings, 1974), p. 105. For all the information on Jigalong, I rely on this report and also on the same author's "Aboriginal Dream Spirit Beliefs in a Contact Situation," *Australian Aboriginal Anthropology*, ed. by R. M. Berndt (Perth: University of Western Australia Press, 1970), pp. 277–91. Dr. Tonkinson writes that the injections are favored because they "are believed to be particularly powerful healing agents." I suggest that some of their own practices and beliefs conditioned them for such treatment. Aborigines are accustomed to having veins, the subincised penis, and the nasal septum pierced by sharp pointed

"instruments," while other parts of the body are cut with sharpened blades (of stone, steel, or shell). Very often such piercing and cutting are not just traditional; they are ritual acts of mythological and sacred significance.

8. Tonkinson, "Aboriginal Dream Spirit Beliefs," pp. 280–81. Tonkinson, *Aboriginal Victors*, pp. 78–79.
9. This summary is based on information from (1) a paper prepared by Dr. B. Whittenbury, District Medical Officer, Alice Springs, February 21, 1975; (2) Dr. Dayalan Devanesen, Department of Health, Alice Springs, who (in July 1976) kindly answered my inquiries and also sent me relevant material; and (3) Pastor Laurie Reece through correspondence (October 2, 1973, and August 2, 1976). As a missionary among the Walbiri (Wailbri), especially at Warrabri, and as a successful student of their language, Mr. Reece helped Doctors Whittenbury and G. E. E. White in their efforts to obtain the cooperation of traditional healers. Mr. Ken Hansen, a member of the Summer Institute of Linguistics, assisted Dr. White in his consultation with the Pintubi in October-November 1971. (L. Reece is author of *Grammar of the Wailbri Language of Central Australia*, Oceania Linguistic Monograph no. 13, and *Dictionary of the Wailbri (Walpiri) Language of Central Australia*, Oceania Linguistic Monograph no. 19.)
10. The linguist, Mrs. Mary Laughren, did not comment on the possible source of the blood that the doctor-man spat out, let alone the pus. The former was probably caused by pressing with his tongue a small sharp flake into his gum or palate. The pus was an illusion arising from the mixed blood and saliva, aided by the release of pressure in her hand as he sucked it. (Cf. J. E. Cawte and M. A. Kidson, "Australian Ethnopsychiatry: The Walbiri Doctor," *Medical Journal of Australia* 2, no. 25 [1964]: 979.)
11. For example, Dennis Gray, anthropologist, West Australian Community Health Services: "Aboriginal Mortuary Practices in Carnarvon," *Oceania* 47, no. 2 (1976).

    I wrote in 1935 that even civilized natives continue to hold magical, mystical, and animistic views regarding illness and death and the treatment of the former. I referred to Aborigines in northeast South Australia, the north coast of New South Wales ("where we should expect that bone-pointing and other magical procedures had gone forever"), and to those on cattle stations in the south of Cape York Peninsula, North Queensland (where R. L. Sharp had just reported that "the belief in the magical causation of illness and accidents was more firmly established than ever"). A. P. Elkin, "Civilized Aborigines and Native Culture," *Oceania* 6, no. 2 (1935): 129–32.
12. A sorcerer, wearing "shoe-pads" made of small emu feathers to disguise his tracks but really to strike terror in the minds of those who see the tracks. Spencer and Gillen, *Native Tribes*, pp. 476, 485. Elkin, *Australian Aborigines*, 5th ed., 1974, pp. 313–15 (1st ed., 1938, pp. 208–10).

13. Dennis Gray, in a letter of March 10, 1976.
14. W. E. H. Stanner, "The Daly River Tribes," p. 25. He added that the doctor "becomes so by associating in dreams with the spirits of the dead." Moreover, he loses his power to cure if he stops dreaming about those spirits.
15. Bungguni, the last of the old-time doctors, is now (1976) too old to "practice." (See chapter 5, note 5). Personal communication from Mr. H. Coate, who has known these tribes for forty years, both in their own territories and at Mowanjum.
16. Cawte, "Tjimi and Tjagolo," pp. 171, 186.
17. R. M. and C. H. Berndt, *Man, Land and Myth in North Australia, the Gunwinggu People* (Sydney: Ure Smith, 1970), pp. 145–46. These anthropologists have been in personal touch with the Gunwinggu for three decades. According to Lamilami (L. Lamilami, *Lamilami Speaks: An Autobiography* [Sydney: Ure Smith, 1974], p. 134) from the Maung tribe on the north of the Gunwinggu, there were no clever men left in 1969, when he was recording his autobiography. Such men formerly passed on their power to their sons. This included predicting the future and curing the sick. For an earlier account of the western Arnhem Land situation, see C. H. Berndt, "The Role of Native Doctors in Aboriginal Australia," in Ari Kiev, ed., *Magic, Faith, and Healing, Studies in Primitive Psychiatry Today* (London: Free Press of Glencoe, 1964), pp. 264–82.
18. Cawte and Kidson, "Australian Ethnopsychiatry," pp. 981–82.
19. This was the situation as I saw it during fieldwork in 1930. But migration from the tribal territories south and southwest of the Aranda had been going on for decades. See A. P. Elkin, "R. H. Mathews: His Contribution to Aboriginal Studies," *Oceania* 46, no. 3 (1976): 214, 218–20.
20. East of the Pidjina (the name for the Pidjandja-djara used in 1930 and earlier by the few white men who had anything to do with them), the Jankundja-djara (eastern Musgraves to the Everard Ranges) and the Andakarinya were in this same arc of tribes. A. P. Elkin, "Kinship in South Australia," *Oceania* 10, no. 2:202, 204.
21. F. G. G. Rose, *The Wind of Change in Central Australia* (Berlin: Akademie-Verlag, 1965), pp. 86, 135. Professor Rose thought another man was also a doctor.
22. This is made possible by the provision of bores and pensions by the government and the use of trucks to bring out stores.
23. Peter Brokensha, *The Pitjantjatjara and their Crafts*, pp. 11, 17, 19, 35. Also, Annette Hamilton, "Socio-Cultural Factors in Health among the Pitjantjatjara," pp. 1–18.
24. Lockwood, *I, the Aboriginal*, pp. 231–35.
25. Ibid., pp. 226–28.
26. Waipuldanya attended in 1957 a conference in Noumea on hygiene among native peoples. He was impressed by one lecturer who "told us in great de-

tail how native medical assistants could help in promoting health and hygiene among their own people." The lecturer also gave sound advice on getting the cooperation of tribal witch doctors. Lockwood, *I, the Aboriginal*, pp. 218–19.

27. R. L. Pulsford and J. Cawte, *Health in a Developing Country* (Brisbane: Jacaranda, 1972).
28. Groote Eylandt Aborigines are said not to have the concept of medicine men. As the need for their help is present, "so-called medicine men in Arnhem Land are brought across to treat the ill. They do so for a fee." Medical Journal of Australia, *Special Supplement on Aboriginal Health* 2, no. 4 (1975): 20.
29. Cawte, "Tjimi and Tjagolo," pp. 187–88. Cawte, *Medicine Is the Law: Studies in Psychiatric Anthropology of Australian Tribal Societies* (Honolulu, University Press of Hawaii, 1974).
30. Cawte and Kidson, "Australian Ethnopsychiatry," p. 981.
31. Correspondence from Dr. D. Devanesen, July 7 and 13, 1976.
32. Cawte and Kidson, ibid.
33. Meggitt, "Djanba among the Walbiri," p. 391.
34. The several spirit-familiars act each according to special diagnosis. One leaves the doctor-man's body to search, over long distances if necessary, for the patient's stolen or lost soul. A second leaves him through the hole in his tongue and enters the patient's body during the sucking procedure to locate the object that had been projected magically into it. This is sucked out with the blood (actually from the doctor-man's tongue) and materializes in the object, which he then displays. A third spirit-familiar works through his fingers to "settle" a patient's disturbed soul. (Information from a draft paper by, and through personal correspondence with, Dr. R. D. Morice, who was in charge of psychiatric services in Central Australia during 1974–75. Dr. Morice spent one week a month with Pintubi and Loritja groups at Kunkiyunti [Brown's Bore] out from Haasts Bluff. I thank Dr. Morice and also Dr. Devanesen, who drew my attention to the former's draft paper.)
35. Roth, *Superstition, Magic*, p. 30.
36. Elkin, Field Notes, 1946. In the latter, the Kalkadoon and Maitakudi tribes, the doctor-man produced the cord from his stomach. It took him quickly where he wanted to go, for example, to a spirit tree, especially when the moon was down, where he heard the spirits of the dead corroboree. This was in response to the song of the mussel shell.
37. Lamilami, *Lamilami Speaks*, p. 124.
38. Cawte, "Tjimi and Tjagolo," pp. 185–86. This incident occurred at Kalumburu Mission, Northern Kimberley.
39. Mrs. Lester died in 1975.

Bibliography

Note: The publication listed throughout this bibliography as *Journal of the Royal Anthropological Institute* has apparently been known by three titles during its existence: before 1907, *Journal Anthropological Institute of Great Britian and Ireland;* from 1907 to 1965, volumes 37–95, *Journal of the Royal Anthropological Institute of Great Britain and Ireland;* and after 1965, simply *Man.*

Angas, G. F. *Savage Life and Scenes in Australia and New Zealand.* London: Smith Elder, 1847.

Basedow, H. *The Australian Aboriginal.* Adelaide: F. W. Preece, 1925.

Bates, D. "The Marriage Laws and Some Customs of the West Australian Aborigines." *Victorian Geographical Journal* 23 (1905).

Baudouin, C. *Suggestion and Auto-Suggestion.* Hackensack, N.J.: Wehmar Bros., 1922.

Berndt, C. H. "The Role of Native Doctors in Aboriginal Australia." In Ari Kiev, ed., *Magic, Faith, and Healing, Studies* in *Primitive Psychiatry Today.* London: Free Press of Glencoe, 1964.

Berndt, R. M. "Wuradjeri Magic and 'Clever Men,'" Parts I and II. *Oceania* 17, 18 (1946–47, 1947–48).

———, ed. *Australian Aboriginal Anthropology.* Perth: University of Western Australia Press, 1970.

Berndt, R. M., and Berndt, C. H. *Man, Land, and Myth in North Australia, the Gunwinggu People.* Sydney: Ure Smith, 1970.

———. "A Preliminary Report of Field-Work in the Ooldea Region." *Oceania* 14, no. 1.

———. Unpublished report on the Wiradjeri.

———. *The World of the First Australians.* Sydney: Ure Smith, 1964.

Berndt and Vogelsang. "The Initiation of Native Doctors in the Dieri Tribe, South Australia." *Records of the South Australian Museum* 6.

Beveridge, P. *The Aborigines of Victoria and the Riverina.* Melbourne: M. L. Hutchinson, 1889.

Bhagavad Gita, trans. L. D. Barnett. London: Temple Classics, 1941.

Bonney, C. "On Some Customs of the Aborigines of the River Darling." *Journal of the Royal Anthropological Institute* 13 (1884).

Bowler, S. C. R. "Aboriginal Customs." *Science of Man* 4.

Brown, A. R. "Notes on the Social Organization of Australian Tribes." *Journal of the Royal Anthropological Institute* 48 (1918).

Bulmer, J. "Some Account of the Aborigines of the Lower Murray, Wimmera, Gippsland and Maneroo." *Victorian Geographical Journal* 5.

Cameron, A. L. P. "Notes on Some Tribes of New South Wales." *Journal of the Anthropological Institute* 14 (1885).

Capell, A. "Mythology in Northern Kimberley, North-West Australia." *Oceania* 9, no. 4.

———. "The Walbiri through Their Own Eyes." *Oceania* 23 (1952–53).

Castaneda, Carlos. *The Teachings of Don Juan—A Yaqui Way of Knowledge.* Harmondsworth: Penguin, 1970.

Cawte, J. E. *Medicine Is the Law: Studies in Psychiatric Anthropology of Australian Tribal Societies.* Honolulu: University Press of Hawaii, 1974.

———. "Tjimi and Tjagolo: Ethnopsychiatry in the Kalumburu People of North-Western Australia." *Oceania* 34 (1963–64).

Cawte, J. E., and Kidson, M. A. "Australian Ethnopsychiatry: The Walbiri Doctor." *Medical Journal of Australia* 2, no. 25 (1964).

Coate, H. H. J. "The Rai and the Third Eye." *Oceania* 38 (1966).

Collins, D. *An Account of the English Colony in New South Wales.* London: T. Cadell and W. Davies, 1798–1802.

Curr, E. M. *The Australian Race.* Melbourne: J. Ferres, Government Printer, 1886–87.

Curr, E. M. *Recollections of Squatting in Victoria.* Melbourne: George Robertson, 1883.

David-Neel, Alexandra. *With Mystics and Magicians in Tibet.* Harmondsworth: Penguin.

Dawson, James. *Australian Aborigines, The Language and Customs of Several Tribes.* Melbourne: G. Robertson, 1881.

Dawson, W. R. "Mummification in Australia and in America." *Journal of the Royal Anthropological Institute* 58 (1928).

Eliade, Mircea. *Australian Religions: An Introduction.* Ithaca, N.Y.: Cornell University Press, 1973.

———. *Shamanism: Archaic Techniques of Ecstasy,* trans. W. R. Trask. Princeton, N. J.: Princeton University Press, 1964.

Elkin, A. P. *The Australian Aborigines: How to Understand Them,* 4th ed. Sydney: Angus & Robertson, 1964; 5th ed., 1974.

———. "Beliefs and Practices Connected with Death in North-eastern and Western South Australia." *Oceania* 7, no. 3.

———. "Burial Practices in North-Eastern and Western South Australia." *Oceania* 7, no. 3.

———. "Civilized Aborigines and Native Culture." *Oceania* 6, no. 2 (1935).

———. "Kinship in South Australia." *Oceania* 10, no. 2.

———. "Notes on the Psychic Life of the Australian Aborigines." *Mankind* 2, no. 3 (1937).

———. "Primitive Medicine Men." *Medical Journal of Australia* (November 30, 1935).

———. "Religion and Philosophy of the Australian Aborigines." In E. C. B. MacLaurin, ed., *Essays in Honour of G. W. Thatcher.* Sydney: Sydney University Press, 1967.

———. "R. H. Mathews: His Contribution to Aboriginal Studies." *Oceania* 46, no. 3 (1976).

———. "Ritual Distribution in Australia." *Oceania* 16, no. 1.

———. "The Social Organization of South Australian Tribes." *Oceania* 2, no. 1.

———. *Studies in Australian Totemism,* Oceania Monograph 2.

Evans-Wentz, W.Y. *Tibetan Yoga and Secret Doctrines.* Oxford: Oxford University Press, 1935 and 1958.

———. *Tibet's Great Yogi, Milarepa,* 2nd ed. Oxford: Oxford University Press, 1969.

Eyre, E. J. *Journals of Expeditions of Discovery into Central Australia.* London: T. & W. Boone, 1845.

Fison, L., and Howitt, A. W. *Kamilaroi and Kurnai.* Melbourne: G. Robertson, 1880.

Fraser, J., ed. *An Australian Language.* Sydney: Sydney Government Printer, 1892.

Freud, Sigmund. *Totem and Taboo,* trans. R. R. Brill. London: Routledge, 1919.

Gason, S. "The Dieyerie Tribe." In J. D. Woods, ed., *The Native Tribes of*

South Australia. Adelaide: E. S. Wigg, 1879.

Gray, Dennis. "Aboriginal Mortuary Practices in Carnarvon." *Oceania* 47, no. 2 (1976).

Greenway, C. C. "Australian Language and Traditions." *Journal of the Royal Anthropological Institute* 7.

Grey, G. *Journals of Two Expeditions of Discovery in Northwestern and Western Australia.* London: T. & W. Boone, 1841.

Gunson, N., ed. *Australian Reminiscences and Papers of L. E. Threlkeld.* Canberra: Australian Institute of Aboriginal Studies, 1974.

Howitt, A. W. *The Native Tribes of South-East Australia.* London: Macmillan, 1904.

———. "On Some Australian Ceremonies of Initiation." *Journal of the Royal Anthropological Institute* 13 (1884).

Howitt, M. E. B. "Some Native Legends from Central Australia." *Folklore* 13 (1902).

Kaberry, P. *Aboriginal Woman, Sacred and Profane.* London: George Routledge, 1939.

Kiev, Ari, ed. *Magic, Faith, and Healing, Studies in Primitive Psychiatry Today.* London: Free Press of Glencoe, 1964.

Lamilami, L. *Lamilami Speaks: An Autobiography.* Sydney: Ure Smith, 1974.

Lockwood, Douglas. *I, the Aboriginal.* Adelaide: Rigby, 1962.

Lumholz, C. *Among Cannibals.* London: M. L. Hutchinson, 1889.

Maddock, Kenneth. *The Australian Aborigines: A Portrait of Their Society.* Harmondsworth: Penguin, 1972.

Mathew, J. *Two Representative Tribes of Queensland.* London: T. Fisher Unwin, 1910.

Mathews, R. H. "The Bora of the Kamilaroi Tribes." *Royal Society of Victoria* 9 (1896).

———. "The Burbung of the Wiradthuri Tribes." *Journal of the Royal Anthropological Institute* 25, 26 (1896, 1897).

———. *Ethnological Notes on the Aboriginal Tribes of New South Wales and Victoria.* Sydney: F. W. White, Printer, 1905.

———. "The Group Divisions and Initiation Ceremonies of the Barkunjee Tribes." *Royal Society of New South Wales* 32.

McConnel, Ursula H. "Mourning Ritual Among the Tribes of Cape York Peninsula." *Oceania* 7, no. 3.

McDougall, A. C. "Manners, Customs and Legends of the Coombangree Tribe." *Science of Man* 3.

McElroy, W. A. "Psi-Testing in Arnhemland." *Oceania* 26 (1955–56).

Medical Journal of Australia. *Special Supplement on Aboriginal Health* 2, no. 4 (1975).

Meggitt, M. J. "Djanba among the Walbiri, Central Australia." *Anthropos* 50 (1955).

Meyer, H. E. A. "The Encounter Bay Tribe." In J. D. Woods, ed., *The Native Tribes of South Australia.* Adelaide: E. S. Wigg, 1879.

Moran, H. M. *Viewless Winds.* London: P. Davies, 1939.

Newland, S. "The Parkengees or Aboriginal Tribes on the Darling River." *South Australian Geographical Journal* 2 (1887–88).

Palmer, E. "Concerning Some Superstitions of North Queensland Aborigines." *Royal Society of Queensland* 2 (1885).

———. "Notes on Some Australian Tribes." *Journal of the Royal Anthropological Institute* 13.

Parker, K. L. *The Euahlayi Tribe.* London: Constable, 1905.

———. *More Australian Legendary Tales.* London: Nutt, 1898.

Pulsford, R. L., and Cawte, J. E. *Health in a Developing Country.* Brisbane: Jacaranda, 1972.

Radcliffe-Brown, A. R. *Social Organization of Australian Tribes.* Oceania Monograph no. 1.

Radin, P. *Primitive Religion: Its Nature and Origin.* London: Dover, 1937.

Ramsay Smith, W. *Myths and Legends of the Australian Aboriginals.* London: G. G. Harrap, 1930.

Reece, Laurie. *Dictionary of the Wailbri (Walpiri) Language of Central Australia.* Oceania Linguistic Monograph no. 19.

———. *Grammar of the Wailbri Language of Central Australia.* Oceania Linguistic Monograph no. 13.

Ridley, W. *Kamilaroi and Other Australian Languages,* 2nd ed. Sydney: 1875.

Rose, F. G. G. *The Wind of Change in Central Australia.* Berlin: Akademie-Verlag, 1965.

Roth, W. E. *Ethnological Studies among the North-West-Central Queensland Aborigines.* Brisbane: Government Printer, 1897.

———. *Superstition, Magic and Medicine.* North Queensland Ethnography Bulletin no. 5, 1903.

Salvado, R. *Memoires historiques sur l'Australie, traduits de l'italien en français par l'abbé Falsimagne.* Paris, 1854.

Sharp, W. L. "Ritual Life and Economics of the Yir-Yoront." *Oceania* 5, no. 1.

Siebert, O. "Sagen und Sitten der Dieri und Nachbarstamme in Zentral-Australien." *Globus* 92 (1910).

Spencer, B., and Gillen, F. J. *The Arunta.* London: Macmillan, 1927.

———. *Native Tribes of Central Australia.* London: Macmillan, 1899.

———. *Northern Tribes of Central Australia.* London: Macmillan, 1904.

———. *Wanderings in Wild Australia,* vol. 1. London: Macmillan, 1928.

Stanner, W. E. H. "The Daly River Tribes." *Oceania* 4, no.1.

———. "On Aboriginal Religion, Part I." *Oceania* 30 (1959).

Strehlow, T. G. H. *Songs of Central Australia.* Sydney: Angus & Robertson, 1971.

Sutton, J. M. "The Adjahdurah Tribe of Aborigines on Yorke's Peninsula." *South Australian Geographical Journal* 2 (1887–88).

Taplin, G. "The Narrinyeri." In J. D. Woods, ed., *The Native Tribes of South Australia.* Adelaide: E. S. Wigg, 1879.

Threlkeld, L. "An Australian Grammar." In J. Fraser, ed., *An Australian Language.* Sydney: Sydney Government Printer, 1892.

Tindale, N. B. "Distribution of Australian Aboriginal Tribes." *Transactions of the Royal Society,* S. A., 64.

Tonkinson, Robert. "Aboriginal Dream Spirit Beliefs in a Contact Situation." In R. M. Berndt, ed., *Australian Aboriginal Anthropology.* Perth: University of Western Australia Press, 1970.

———. *The Aboriginal Victors of* the *Desert Crusade.* Cummings, 1974.

Tyrrell, G. N. M. *Science and Psychical Phenomena.* London: Methuen, 1938.

Warner, W. L. *A Black Civilization, A Social Study of an Australian Tribe.* New York: Harper, 1937.

Webb, T. T. "The Making of a Marrngit." *Oceania* 6, no. 3.

Wilhelmi, C. "Manners and Customs of the Australian Natives, in Particular of the Port Lincoln District." *Royal Society of Victoria* 5 (1862).

Williams, F. E. *Papuans of the Trans-Fly.* Oxford: Oxford University Press, 1936.

Woods, J. D., ed. *The Native Tribes of South Australia.* Adelaide: E. S. Wigg, 1879.

Worms, Ernest. "Aboriginal Place Names in Kimberley, Western Australia." *Oceania* 14, no. 4.

Index

Books of Related Interest

Voices of the First Day
Awakening in the Aboriginal Dreamtime
by Robert Lawlor

Wise Women of the Dreamtime
Aboriginal Tales of the Ancestral Powers
by K. Langloh Parker
Edited by Johanna Lambert

Men's Business, Women's Business
The Spiritual Role of Gender in the World's Oldest Culture
by Hannah Rachel Bell

The Speaking Land
Myth and Story in Aboriginal Australia
by Ronald M. Berndt and Catherine H. Berndt

Kahuna of Light
The World of Hawaiian Spirituality
by Moke Kupihea

Original Wisdom
Stories of an Ancient Way of Knowing
by Robert Wolff

Spirit of the Shuar
Wisdom from the Last Unconquered People of the Amazon
by John Perkins and Shakaim Mariano Shakai Ijisam Chumpi

Star Ancestors
Indian Wisdomkeepers Share the Teachings of the Extraterrestrials
by Nancy Red Star